THE LURE OF THE PEN

A BOOK FOR WOULD-BE AUTHORS

Every aspiring author hopes to become a published professional, but there are many pitfalls on the way. For every writer who successfully manages to get an article published, either fiction or fact, there are literally hundreds who tried and failed.

Emily Flora Klickmann was an English journalist, author, and editor. She was the editor of the "*Girl's Own Paper*" for 23 years, from 1908 to 1931, as well as publishing numerous novels, advice books, children's stories, and non-fiction on many topics including gardening, cooking, and needlework techniques.

From her unique position as both an editor and writer, her book "*The Lure of the Pen*," provides the beginning writer with the advice and perspective needed to make the right decisions in creating an article or novel that is ready for publication.

For the fiction writer she doesn't merely point out what needs to be done to make believable characters and situations, but also what needs to be avoided, such as "peculiarity is not originality" and "slang is quickly out-dated."

Similarly, for the writer who specializes in the real world, she shows examples of how not to write an article (editors do not want repeat-subjects, verbosity is boring), as well as what will work in preparing a finished piece that is of interest not only to the editor, but also to the eventual reader (topicality is important, there is a time lag between when a magazine buys an article and when it is actually published).

For both writers, she offers advice on how to deal with an editor, what is reasonable to expect, what is not. For example, one of the surest ways to fail at getting published is to insult the editor, his magazine, or his company, and Flora Klickmann points out how many aspiring writers do this without even realizing it.

If you're trying to get what you write published, following Flora Klickmann's advice is a good start.

Flora Klickmann was born on January 26, 1867 in Brixton, London, one of six children. As a girl she aspired to be a concert pianist, but suffered from illness in her teens and at the age of 21 began work as a music teacher. She then moved into music journalism, and by 1895 had started contributing articles to *The Windsor Magazine*, one of the best-known story periodicals of the time. In 1904, she became the editor of *The Foreign Field*. By this time, she had also begun writing and editing books on crafts and etiquette, aimed at young girls.

Four years later, in 1908, she was appointed editor of the *Girl's Own Paper*, a highly successful periodical aimed at girls and young women published by the Religious Tract Society (RTS). She introduced new themes such as careers advice for girls, advice on style and dress, photography competitions and crafts. Long serials became less common, replaced by a shorter stories, often from distant parts of the world.

In 1912 she suffered a breakdown through overwork and stress. While remaining as editor, she spent a period of convalescence in the Wye valley, an area in which her grandparents had lived. In 1913, she married Ebenezer Henderson Smith, one of the executives at the RTS.

In 1916 she began publishing written sketches of life in her country cottage at Brockweir, with its idyllic cottage garden and spectacular views over the River Wye and Tintern Abbey. The book, *The Flower-Patch Among the Hills*, was highly successful. In later years the stories grew to involve her household and the local people, combining nature description, anecdote, autobiography, religion, and humour. In all, seven *Flower Patch* books were published, over 32 years. Her writing has been described as "humorous, elegant and beautifully observed, revealing a genuine love and concern for the natural world."

She also published novels, advice books, children's stories and non-fiction on many topics including gardening, cooking, and needlework techniques. She remained editor of the *Girl's Own Paper* until 1931.

Her husband died in 1937. She died in 1958, and was buried in the graveyard of the Moravian Church at Brockweir.

THE LURE OF THE PEN

A BOOK FOR WOULD-BE AUTHORS

By Flora Klickmann

Flying Chipmunk Publishing
Bennington, NH

This is a reprint of a book originally published in 1920, first in Great Britain, then in the United States. Every effort has been made to ensure the accuracy of the reprint, although there have been minor changes to correct archaic spellings, such as changing "dulness" to "dullness."

THE LURE OF THE PEN
A BOOK FOR WOULD-BE AUTHORS

by Flora Klickmann
Editing and Format Copyright © 2011 by Terry Kepner.

THE LURE OF THE PEN
A BOOK FOR WOULD-BE AUTHORS

Published by Flying Chipmunk Publishing
162 Onset Road
Bennington, NH 03442

ISBN: 978-1-61720-124-0
             1-61720-124-3

Cover Design by Terry Kepner
First Flying Chipmunk Publishing edition: September 2011.

DEDICATED TO

MR. JAMES BOWDEN

WHO HAS FEW EQUALS, EITHER

AS A PUBLISHER, OR AS A FRIEND

Table of Contents

The Lure of the Pen
A Book for Would-Be Authors

Preface to the American Edition

In sending out this new book to the American public, I feel I am addressing a sympathetic audience, since other volumes that have preceded it have been most cordially received, and have added considerably to my long list of friends on the Western side of the Atlantic.

At first glance it may seem as though the difference between the writings of American and British authors is too marked to allow of a book on Authorship proving useful to both countries—but in reality the difference is only superficial, and is largely confined to methods of newspaper journalism, or connected with mannerisms and topical qualities.

Fundamentally, both nations work on the same lines and acknowledge the same governing laws in Literature. American authors, no less than British, derive their inspirations from European classics.

And magazine editors and publishers in both countries are only too grateful for good work from either side.

No one can teach authors how or what to write; but sometimes it is possible to help the beginners to an understanding of what it is better not to write. For the rest I hope the book explains itself.

FLORA KLICKMANN
Fleet Street, London.

PART ONE

The Mss. That Fail

In the Business of Making Literature,
the only Quality that presents itself in Abundance
is entirely untrained Mediocrity.

The Lure of the Pen

Why They Fail

In the course of a year I read somewhere about nine thousand stories, articles and poems. These are exclusive of those read by others in my office.

Of these nine thousand I purchase about six hundred per annum. The remainder are usually declined for one of three reasons; either,

They are not suited to the policy and the requirements of the publishing house, or the periodicals, for which I am purchasing. Or,

They tread ground we have already covered. Or,

They have no marketable value.

The larger proportion of the rejected Mss. come under the last heading. They are of the "homing" order, warranted to return to their starting point.

The number that I buy does not indicate the number that I require. In normal times I could use at any rate double the number that I purchase. I never have an overstock of the right thing. I never have more than I can publish of certain-to-sell matter. No publisher or editor ever has.

In the business of Making Literature (and throughout these chapters I use the word literature in its widest sense) genius is rare. Nearly-genius is almost as rare. The only quality that presents itself in abundance is entirely untrained mediocrity.

It may be thought that this applies equally to all departments of the world's work; but it is not so. While genius is scarce wherever one looks, I know of only one other vocation where the candidates expect good pay at the very start without any sort of training, any experience, any specialised knowledge, or any idea of the simplest requirement of the business from which they hope to draw an income—the other vocation being domestic service.

For example: Though thousands of paintings and sketches are offered me in the course of the year, I cannot recall one instance of an artist announcing that this is his, or her, first attempt at drawing; all the work submitted, even the feeblest, shows previous practice or training of some sort, be it ever so elementary. Yet it is no uncommon thing to receive with a Ms. a letter explaining, "This is the first time I have ever tried to write anything."

Then again, no one expects to be engaged to play a violin solo at a concert, when she has had no training, merely because she craves a public appearance and applause. Yet many a girl and woman writes to an editor: "This is my first attempt at a poem. I do so hope you will publish it, as I should so like to see myself in print."

And no one would expect to get a good salary as a dressmaker by announcing that, though she has not the most elementary knowledge of the business, she feels convinced that she could make a dress. Yet over and over again people have asked me to give them a chance, explaining that, though they were quite inexperienced, they felt they had it in them to write.

Nevertheless, despite this prevailing idea that we all possess heaven-sent genius, which is ready to sprout and blossom straight away with no preparatory work—an idea which gains added weight from the fact that there are no great schools for the student who desires to enter the literary profession, as there are for students of art and music—some training is imperative; and if the would-be writer is to go far, the training must be rigorous and very comprehensive.

But unlike most other businesses and professions, the novice must train himself; he can look for very little help from others.

The art student gains information and experience by working with others in a studio; it gives him some common ground for comparisons; where all are sketching from the same model, he is able to see work that is better, and work that is worse, than his own; and probably he is able to grasp wherein the difference lies.

The music student who is one of several to remain in the room while each in turn has a pianoforte lesson, hears the remarks of the professor (possibly a prominent man in his own profession) on each performance, and can learn a large amount from the criticisms and corrections bestowed on the others, quite apart from those applying to her own playing.

But for the would-be author there is no college where the leading literary lights listen patiently, for an hour or two at a stretch, while the students read their stories and poems and articles aloud for criticism and correction. Here and there ardent amateurs form themselves into small literary coteries for this purpose; but often these either develop into mutual admiration societies, or fizzle out for lack of a guiding force.

LITERATURE IS THE MOST ELUSIVE BUSINESS IN THE WORLD

The difficulty with literature is this: It is the most elusive business in the world. No one can say precisely what constitutes good literature, because, no matter how you may classify and tabulate its characteristics, some new genius is sure to break out in a fresh place; and no one can lay down a definite course of training that can be relied on to meet even the average requirements of the average case.

You can set the instrumentalist to work at scales and studies for technique; the dressmaker can practise stitchery and the application of scientific measurement; the art student can study the laws governing perspective, balance of design, the juxtaposition of colour, and a dozen other topics relative to his art.

And more than this, in most businesses (and I include the professions) you can demonstrate to the students, in a fairly convincing manner, when their work is wrong. You can show the girl who is learning dressmaking the difference between large uneven stitches and small regular ones; the undesirability of having a skirt two inches longer at one side than it is at the other. You can indicate to the art student when his subject is out of drawing, or suggest a preferable choice of colours. And though these points may only touch the mechanical surface of things, they help the student along the right road, and are invaluable aids to him in his studies. True, such advice cannot make good a lack of real genius, yet it may help to develop nearly-genius, and that is not to be despised.

But with literature, there is so little that is tangible, and so much that is intangible. Beyond the bare laws that govern the construction of the language, only a fraction of the knowledge that is necessary can be stated in concrete terms for the guidance of the student. And because it is difficult to reduce the art of writing to any set of rules, the amateur often regards it as the one vocation that is entirely devoid of any constructive principles; the one vocation wherein each can do exactly as he pleases, and be a law unto himself, no one being in a better position than himself to say what is great and what is feeble, since no one else can quote chapter and verse as authority for making a pronouncement on the merits—and more particularly the demerits—of his work.

And yet, nearly all the English-speaking race want to write. The craving for "self-expression" is one of the characteristics of this century; and what better medium is there for this than writing? Hence the lure of the pen.

It is partly because so many beginners do not know where to turn for criticism, or an opportunity to measure their work with that of others, that some send their early, crude efforts to editors, hoping to get, at least, some opinion or word of guidance, even though the Ms. be declined. Yet this is what an editor cannot undertake to do. Think what an amount of work would be involved if I were to set down my reasons for declining each of those eight thousand and more Mss. that I turn down annually! It could not be done, in addition to all the other claims on one's office time.

Why the Mss. are Rejected

But though life would be too short for any editor to write even a brief criticism on each Ms. rejected, certain defects repeat themselves so often that it is quite possible to specify some outstanding faults—or rather, qualities which are lacking—that lead to the downfall of one Ms. after another, with the automatic persistency of recurring decimals.

Speaking broadly, I generally find that the Ms. which is rejected because it has no marketable value betrays one or more of the following deficiencies in its author:—

Lack of any preliminary training.
  "   "   specialised knowledge of the subject dealt with.
  "   "   modernity of thought and diction.
  "   "   the power to reduce thought to language.
  "   "   cohesion and logical sequence of ideas.
  "   "   ability to get the reader's view-point.
  "   "   new and original ideas and themes.
  "   "   the instinct for selection.
  "   "   a sense of proportion.

The majority of such defects can be remedied with study and practice; and even though the final result may not be a work of genius, it will be something much more likely to be marketable than the Ms. that has neither knowledge nor training behind it.

THREE ESSENTIALS IN TRAINING

"How am I to set about training for literary work?" is a question that is put to me most days in the year.

Training comes under three headings: Observation, Reading, and Writing.

The majority of beginners make the mistake of putting writing first; but before you can commit anything to paper, you must have something in your head to write down. If you have but little in your brain, your writing will be worthless.

WE GET OUT OF LIFE WHAT WE PUT INTO IT

Just as a plant requires special fertilisers if it is to develop fine blossoms and large fruit, so the mind requires food of exceptional nourishment if it is to produce something out of the ordinary, something worth reading.

It is one of the great laws of Nature that, as a general rule, we get out of life about what we put into it. If a farmer wants bumper crops, he must apply manure liberally to his land; if a man wants big returns from his business, he must devote much time and thought and energy to it. And in the same way, if you want good stuff to come out of your head, you must first of all put plenty of good stuff in.

But—and this is very important—it is not supposed to come out again in the same form that it went in! This point beginners often forget. When sweet peas are fed with sulphate of ammonia, they don't promptly produce more sulphate of ammonia; they utilise the chemical food to promote much finer and altogether better flowers. The same principle governs the application of suitable nourishment to all forms of life—the recipient retains its own personal characteristics, but transmutes the food into the power to intensify, enlarge, and develop those personal characteristics.

In like manner, the food you give your mind must be used to intensify and enlarge and develop your individuality; and what you write must reflect your individuality (not to be confused with egoism); it should not be merely a paraphrase of your reading.

All this is to explain why I put observation and reading before writing. They are the principal channels through which the mind is fed. And, in the main, the value of your early literary work will be in direct ratio to the keenness and accuracy of your observation, and the wisdom shown in your choice of reading.

You think this sounds like reducing writing to a purely mechanical process, in which genius does not count?

Not at all. It is merely that the initial stages of training for any work involve a certain amount of routine and repetition, until we have acquired facility in expressing our ideas.

In any case, very few of us are suffering from real genius. Ability, talent, cleverness, are fairly common; but genius is rare. If you possess genius, you will discover it quite soon, and, what is more important, other people will likewise discover it. As some one has said, "Genius, like murder, *will* out!" You can't hide it.

Meanwhile, it will save time and argument to pretend that you are just an ordinary being like the rest of us, with everything to learn; you will progress more rapidly on these lines than if you spend time contemplating, and admiring, what you think is a Heaven-sent endowment that requires no shaping.

PART TWO

On Keeping Your Eyes Open

One of the drawbacks of an
Advanced Civilisation
is the fact that it tends to
lessen the power of Observation.

A Course in Observation

Begin your observation course by noting anything and everything likely to have a bearing on the subject of your writing, and jot down your observations in the briefest of notes. No matter if it seem a trifling thing, in the early part of your training it will be well worth your while to record even the trifles, since this all helps to develop and focus the faculty for observation.

One of the drawbacks of an advanced civilisation is the fact that it tends to lessen the power of observation. The average person in this twentieth century sees next to nothing of the detail of life. We have no longer the need to cultivate observation for self-protection and food-finding as in primitive times. Everything is done for us by pressing a button or putting a penny in the slot, till it is fast becoming too much of an effort for us even to look (or it was, before the War); and the ability to look—and to see when we look—is, consequently, disappearing through disuse.

You will be surprised how much there is in this practice of observation, once you get started.

Study Human Characteristics

For example: If you intend to write a story, you will need to study the various types of people figuring therein; the distinguishing characteristics, the method of speaking, and the mental attitude of each.

The amateur invariably states the colour of a girl's eyes and hair, and the tint of her complexion, with some sentences about her social standing and her clothes, and then considers her fully equipped for her part in the piece. Whereas, in reality, these items are of no importance so far as a story goes. We really do not mind whether Dinah, in *Adam Bede*, had violet eyes or grey-green; it is the soul of the woman that counts. Neither do we trouble whether Portia wore a well-tailored coat and skirt, or a simple muslin frock lavishly trimmed with Valenciennes; it is her ready wit, her resourcefulness, and her deep-lying affection that interest us.

Next in importance to the human beings are the circumstances involved.

Does your heroine decide to leave her millionaire-father's palatial home and hide her identity in slum-work and a room in a tenement?

You will have to do a fair amount of first-hand observation to get the details and general "atmosphere" appertaining to a millionaire's residence and mode of living, and contrast these with the conditions that represent life in the squalid quarters of a city.

Environment and Circumstances offer Wide Scope

Perhaps you will tell me that it is impossible for you to make these observations, as you do not know your way about any real slum, or you are not on visiting terms with and any millionaire. That raises another important question that I hope to deal with later, when we come to the subject of story-writing. Here I can only say, Don't attempt to write upon topics you are unable to study at near range.

After all, there are unlimited subjects that are close to everybody's hand. You may be including a dog in your story. Is he to be a *real* dog, or that dear, faithful old creature, who has been leading an active life (in fiction) for a century or more, rescuing the heir when he tumbles in a pond; apprising the sleeping family upstairs of the fact that the clothes-horse by the kitchen fire has caught alight; tracking the burglar to his lair; re-uniting fallen-out lovers by sitting up beseechingly on his hind legs, and in a hundred other ways making himself generally useful?

I am fond of dogs, and I never grudge them literary honours; but I sometimes wish we could get a change of descriptive matter where they are concerned. What are *you* proposing to say about the dog? "He ran joyfully to meet his master, wagging his tail the while"? Something like that? I shouldn't wonder. That is the beginning and the end of so many amateur descriptions of a dog; and, judging by the number of times I have read these words, his poor tail must be nearly wagged off by now.

Instead of being content with this, start making careful observations, and you will soon have something else to write about. Notice how a dog talks—with his ears; he can tell you almost anything, once you learn to read his ears. And when you have noted all the points you can in this direction, and mastered this part of his language, see what you can learn from his walk; you can estimate a dog's temper and feelings, his sorrow, his joy, and the state of his health, by noticing the variations in his walk. Why, any one dog can provide you with a book full of observations.

You may say, however, that as your story is to be a short one, you could never use up a book full of observations if you had them.

YOU NEED A SCORE OF FACTS IN YOUR HEAD FOR EACH ONE YOU PUT ON PAPER

Very likely; but always remember that you need to have a score of facts in your head for every one you put down on paper. You must be thoroughly saturated with a subject before you can write even a brief description in a telling and convincing manner. Therefore, never be afraid of making too many notes in your observation-book.

Many of these entries you will never refer to again; the very act of writing them down will so impress them on your memory that they become a matter-of-course to you. This in itself is valuable training; it is one of the processes by which a person may become "well-informed"—an essential qualification for a good writer.

While over-elaboration of detail in your writing is seldom desirable, apart from a text-book or a treatise, knowledge of detail is imperative if that writing is to conjure up situations in the reader's mind and make them seem vividly real. In describing scenery, for instance, you do not need to give the name of every bit of vegetation in sight, till your Ms. looks like a botanical dictionary; but it is useful to know those names, you may require some of them; and until your work is actually shaping, you cannot tell exactly what you will use and what omit.

KEEN OBSERVATION WILL SAVE YOU FROM PITFALLS

The habit of keen observation will save you from a legion of pitfalls. The more you train your eyes to see, and your mind to retain what you have seen, the less chance there is of your putting down inaccuracies.

I have been reading a Ms. wherein the heroine—a beautiful girl with a face like a haunting memory (whatever that may look like)—spent a whole afternoon lying full-length on the grass, the first sunny day in February, revelling in the scent of violets near by, and watching the swallows skimming above her. If the writer had no opportunity to observe the comings and goings of swallows, she might at least have turned up an encyclopædia, when she would have found that swallows do not arrive in England till well on into April.

Then, after 249 more pages, the beautiful girl finally died of a broken heart—obviously absurd! In real life she would have died on the very next page of rheumatic fever and double pneumonia, after lying on the wet grass all that time!

Frequently, when I point out similar errors to the novice, I get some such reply as this, "Of course, that reference to swallows was only a slip of the pen"; or, "After all, it is merely a minor point whether she lay on the grass or walked along the road; it doesn't really affect the story as a whole."

True, such discrepancies may be only minor details; but, on the other hand, they may not. I have noticed, however, that the writer who is inaccurate on small points is equally liable to inaccuracy where the main features of the story are concerned; and the writer who does not know enough about his subject to get his details right seldom knows enough about it to get any of it right.

THE ASSESSMENT OF SPIRITUAL VALUES

There is one aspect of life that can only be learnt by observation; a phase of your training where books and lectures can be of but little assistance to you. Important as it is that you should note the material things relating to your subject, it is still more important that you should train yourself to note the psychological bearings and the spiritual values of life, since these are often of far more vital consequence to a story than the plot.

By "spiritual values" I do not necessarily mean anything of a directly religious quality. I use the term to signify the revelation of mind and heart and soul of the various characters that a writer presents, as distinct from a catalogue of externals; the reading of motives, and the recognition of the forces that are within us, as distinguished from the chronicling of superficial items.

THE UNSEEN THAT COUNTS

So often in the world of men and women around us it is the unseen that counts. Just below the surface life is teeming with motives and aims and ideals

and personality; with problems that involve mixed feelings, and produce paradox and misjudgment, and apparently irreconcilable qualities. These may show
scarcely a ripple on the outside, and yet be the real factors that are shaping lives,
and influencing the world for better or for worse, and, incidentally, affecting the
whole trend of a story.

To gauge these abstract qualities and their consequences accurately is the big-
gest task of the writer; and according to the amount of such insight that he brings
to bear on his subject, will be the durability of his work, since this alone is the
part that lives. Fashions and furniture, scenery and architecture, maps and dynas-
ties, laws and customs, even language and the meaning of words, all change; and
the older grows the world, the more rapid are the changes. The only things that
remain unaltered are the laws of Nature and the longings of the soul. Hence the
only writings that last beyond the changing fashions of the moment are those that
centralise on these fundamental things, giving secondary place to ephemeral details.

If you want your work to live, it is useless to make the main interest centre
in something that will be out-of-date and passed beyond human memory within
a very little while.

This insight as to the subtleties of life is the quality that gives vitality to your
writing. Without it your characters will be no more alive than a wax figure in a
draper's window, no matter how handsomely you may clothe them in descriptive
matter. Have you ever read a story wherein the heroine seemed about as real and
alive as a saw-dust-stuffed doll, and the hero had as much "go" in him as a wooden
horse? I have, alas! thousands of them! And the reason for the lifelessness was the
lack in the author of all sense of "spiritual values."

A knowledge of the inner workings of the mind and heart and soul can only
be acquired by close and constant observation. You may remember in *Julius Cæsar*,
where Cæsar tells Antonio that if he were liable to fear, the man he should avoid
would be Cassius; he describes him thus: "He is a great observer, and he looks
quite through the deeds of men." It is just this power that the writer needs—the
ability to look past the actions themselves to the motives that prompted them.

It is so easy to record the obvious. What we need to look for is the truth that
is not obvious. For instance, at first sight it may seem quite easy for us to decide
why a person did a certain thing. A woman makes an irritable remark. Why did
she make that irritable remark? Bad temper! we promptly reply. But perhaps it
wasn't bad temper; it may have been due to ill-health—a bad tooth can generate as
much irritability in half an hour as the worse temper going. Or it may have been
caused by insomnia; or by nerves strained to the breaking-point with trouble and
anxiety. Or the speaker may have been vexed with herself for some action of her
own, and her vexation found vent in this way.

If you were writing a story, the cause of her irritability might be an important
link in the chain of events. And in scores of other directions, the cause of an
action might be infinitely more important in the working out of your plot than
the action itself.

Moreover, if you want your work to appeal to a wide and varied audience, you must take as your main theme something that is understood by all conditions of people; something that makes a universal appeal. That is why the greatest writers make the human heart the pivot of their stories, as a rule. Readers are primarily interested in the doings of, and the happenings to, certain people; and very particularly the motives that led up to the doings and happenings, and the reasons why certain things were said and done, and the psychological results of the sayings and doings.

THE MAIN THEME SHOULD MAKE A UNIVERSAL APPEAL

In the main, it is not of paramount importance to you, when you are engrossed in a story, whether the scene is laid in Japan among decaying Buddhist temples, or in a Devonshire village. It is the personality of the characters, their sorrows and joys, their struggles and love affairs, and the solution of their human problems that make the chief claim on your interest. Certainly, the scenery and "local colour" and inanimate surroundings may influence you favourably or otherwise—backgrounds and the general "setting" of a story are valuable, more valuable than the amateur realises; nevertheless, they are not the main features, and should never be made the main features in fiction.

Once you grasp the importance of the "spiritual values," in life itself no less than in writing, you will understand why it is that some books survive centuries of change and social upheaval, and appeal to all sorts and conditions of temperaments. When we study Shakespeare at school, we invariably wonder in our secret heart (even though we daren't voice such heresy!) what on earth people can see in him. To our immature intelligence he can be dullness itself, while his style seems long-winded, and many of his plots appear most feeble affairs beside our favourite books of adventure. We are not sufficiently developed and experienced in our school days to be able to understand and appreciate his greatness, which lies in his amazing knowledge of the human heart and his grasp of "spiritual values."

LIFE IS EVER OFFERING NEW DISCOVERIES

One of the fascinating things about life is the way it is for ever offering us new discoveries. We never need get to the end of anything. There are always heights beyond heights, depths below depths, further recesses to penetrate, fresh things to find out. And nowhere is this more clearly demonstrated than when we come to the study of human nature itself. The writer who strives to depict men and women as they really are is always coming on new surprises; he never arrives at the end of his observations. And he soon realises how infinitely more important are the subtle workings of the heart and mind than all the material things that crowd the outside surface of life.

TO WRITE CONVINCINGLY ONE NEEDS SYMPATHY

To be able to write convincingly about people, we must know them; to know them we must live among them, and sympathise with them—for there is no other way to know and understand the human heart. It is very easy to ridicule people's weakness, and make cheap sarcasm over their failings; but it is useless to make your observations with a cynic's smile. The cynic really gets nowhere; he merely robs life of much of its beauty, giving nothing in its place.

To write about people so that we grip the hearts of all who read, it is necessary to look beyond the superficial weaknesses, and below the temporary failings, to that part of humanity that still bears the image of the Divine Creator. And you need sympathy to accomplish this.

Would-be authors often tell me that they are sick of their everyday routine—office work, teaching, nursing, home duties, or whatever it may be—and long to throw it all up so that they may devote all their time to writing.

TO KNOW PEOPLE, WE MUST LIVE AND WORK AMONG THEM

But you cannot devote all of your time to writing! The beginner never understands this. A great deal of an author's time is taken up with the study of people, and a general quest for material for his books.

While you are in the early stages of your writing, it is absolutely necessary for you that you should be doing some sort of other work in company with your fellow-creatures, and experiencing the ordinary routine of life, else how can you possibly get your writing properly balanced and true to life?

If you try to isolate yourself from the everyday happenings of normal existence, avoiding the tiresome duties and the irksome routine, merely keeping your eyes on your Ms., or on yourself, or on only the things that appeal to you, how can you ever expect your work to be in right perspective? Under such conditions what you write would be bound to give an incomplete, incorrect view of life, one-sided, and out of all proper proportion, and—the result could be nothing but a dire failure.

Stay where you are, and make your corner of the universe your special study.

HOW MUCH DO YOU KNOW OF THOSE WHO ARE NEAREST TO YOU?

Perhaps you think you know everything that is to be known about people around you. But do you, I wonder? Do they know everything about you—your ideals and inner struggles, and aims and aspirations?

I doubt it.

Experience shows that very often the people we know least of all are those with whom we come into daily contact. We take them for granted. We do not even trouble to try to understand them. That they should have doubts and difficulties, heart-aches and hopes and high aspirations, even as we have, sometimes comes as a surprise to us.

Begin your observations just where you are now. See if you can find the glint of gold that is always somewhere below the surface in every human being, if we can but strike the right place. Try to sort out the reasons and the motives that are thick in the air around you. See if you can discern another side to a person's character than the one you have always accepted as a matter of course.

And write down your discoveries and your observations. You will need them later on.

Here, then, is the first step in training yourself for authorship. It is only one step, I admit; but you will find it can be made to cover a good deal of ground.

Part Three

The Help That Books Can Give

Steady, quiet, consecutive reading is necessary if we are to do
steady quiet, consecutive thinking; and, without such thinking, it
is impossible for writers to produce anything worth while.

The Bane of "Browsing"

While a wide range of reading, and a general all-round knowledge of standard literature are essential, if you hope to become a writer, there are three directions in which you can specialise with great advantage—reading for definite data, reading for style, and reading for the study of technique, *i.e.* to find out how the author does it.

With such matters as reading for recreation we have nothing to do here. Training for authorship means work, regular work, stiff mental work.

Some amateurs seem to think that a course of desultory dipping into books is a guarantee of literary efficiency, or an indication of literary ability.

"I am never so happy as when I am curled up in an armchair surrounded by books"; or "I do so love to browse among books," girls will tell me, when they are asking if I can find them a post in my office, or on the staff of one of my magazines.

It is so difficult for the uninitiated to understand that the business of writing and making books is one that entails as much close, monotonous work as any other business; and the mere fact that any one spends a certain amount of time in reading a bit here and a bit there, picking up a book for a half-hour's entertainment and throwing it down the minute it ceases to stimulate the curiosity, is no more preparation for literary work than an occasional tinkling at a piano, trying a few bars here and there of chance compositions, would be any preparation for giving a pianoforte recital or composing a sonata.

Nature's Revenge for the Misuse of the Brain

I have nothing to say against dipping into books as a recreation—refreshing one's memory among old friends, or looking for happy discoveries in new-comers—I have passed hosts of pleasant half-hours in this way myself when my brain was too tired to work, and I wanted relaxation. But such reading is not work; neither is it training in any sort of sense—it is merely a pastime; and, as such, must only be taken in moderation. It should be the exception, not a habit.

If you allow yourself to get into this way of haphazard reading, in time you lose the ability to do any consecutive reading, and, as a natural consequence, it would be utterly impossible for you to do any consecutive thinking,—an essential for connected writing.

The reason for this is quite clear, if you think it over. When you persistently skim a legion of books, or dip into them casually, and live mentally on a diet of snippets—a form of reading that has been the vogue of late years—you are giving yourself mental indigestion that is wonderfully akin to the indigestion that would follow a food diet on similar lines. If your meals always consisted of snacks taken at all sorts of odd times—fried fish followed by rich chocolates, with a nibble at a mince tart, a few spoonfuls of preserved ginger, a trifle of roast duck, some macaroni cheese, a little salmon and cucumber, some grouse, oyster patties, and ice-cream on top of that—your stomach wouldn't know what to do with it all, and—— I need say no more about it!

In the same way, when you read first one thing and then another, piling poems on love scenes, then adding a motley, disconnected selection of scraps of information (of doubtful use in most cases) with sensational episodes and pessimistic outpourings, irrespective of any sort of sequence or logical connection, your mind doesn't know what to do with the conglomeration; for no sooner has your thinking machine set one series of thoughts in motion, than it has to switch off that current and start on something else. Eventually the brain gives up the struggle; the thoughts cease to work; you lose the power to remember—much less to assimilate—what you read.

In the end, you can't read! Nature is bound to take this course in sheer self-defence; the only alternative would be lunacy!

WHY SO MANY WANT BOOKS THAT SHRIEK

You can see all this exemplified, pitifully, in the present day. With the great rush of cheap books (and still cheaper education) that flooded the country at the beginning of this century, the masses simply gorged themselves with indiscriminate reading-matter—of a sort, (and so did many who ought to have known better). Gradually they lost the taste for straight-forward simple stories of human life as it really is; things had to be blood-curdling and highly sensational. The type of reading-matter that had formerly been associated solely with the "dime novel" and depraved youths of the criminal class, found its way into all sorts and conditions of bindings, and all sorts and conditions of homes. People's minds were getting so blunted that they simply could not follow anything unless it was punctuated with lurid lights; they could not grasp anything unless it was crude and bizarre and monstrous; they could not hear anything of the Still Small Voice that is the essence of all beauty in literature, art or nature. Everything had to be in shouts and shrieks to arrest their attention.

Finally, the masses lost the power to read at all, and we are now living in an age when everything must be presented in the most obvious medium—pictures. Few people can concentrate on reading even the day's news—it has to be given in pictures. The picture-palace and the music-hall *revue* (which is another form of spectacular entertainment) stand for the mental stimulus that is the utmost a large bulk of the population are equal to to-day.

We delude ourselves by saying that we live in such a busy age, we have not *time* to read. But it is not our lack of time so much as our lack of brain power that is the trouble; and that brain power has been dissipated, primarily, by over-indulgence in desultory reading that was valueless.

All this is to explain why a course of indiscriminate "browsing" is no recommendation for the one who wishes to take up literary work. Steady, quiet, consecutive reading is necessary if we are to do steady, quiet, consecutive thinking; and, without such thinking, it is impossible to write anything worth whiles.

Let your reading extend over a wide range, certainly—the wider the better, so long as you can cover the ground thoroughly—for an author should be well-read.

But take care that you do *read*; don't mistake "nibbling" for reading. Far better know but one poem of Browning thoroughly and understandingly, than have on your shelves a complete set of his works into which you dip at random, when the mood seizes you, with no clear idea as to what any of it is about.

READING FOR DEFINITE DATA

Turning from reading in general to the specialised reading I have suggested—the first heading explains itself. Many subjects that you write upon will require a certain amount of preliminary reading—some a great deal—in order that you may accumulate facts, or get the details of climate and scenery correct, or the mode of life prevalent at a specified time.

Such a book as Mrs. Florence Barclay's novel, *The White Ladies of Worcester*—with the scene laid in the twelfth century—must have necessitated a great deal of research among the historical and church records of that era, and the reading of books bearing on that period, in order to get all the details accurate, and to conjure up as convincingly as the author has done, an all-pervading feeling of the spirit of those times.

All stories dealing with a bygone period require much preliminary reading, in order that one may become imbued with the spirit of that particular age, as well as familiarised with its manners and customs and mode of speech.

Most amateurs seem to think that a plentiful sprinkling of expletives about the pages, with the introduction of a few historic names and events, are sufficient to produce the required old-world atmosphere. I could not possibly count the number of Mss. I have read where the rival suitor for the hand of "Mistress Joan" says "Gadsook" in every other sentence, while the estimable young man who, like her father, is loyal to the king, is hidden away in the secret-panel room.

But tricks such as these do not give the story an authentic atmosphere. You can only get this by systematic study of the literature relating to the period.

And others, besides novelists, find it advantageous to study historical records. I remember when Mr. William Canton (the author of those charming studies of child life, *W. V., Her Book*, and *The Invisible Playmate*) was engaged on the big history of the British and Foreign Bible Society, and was writing the account of the Society's Bible work in Italy, not only did he read all their official reports, and the correspondence bearing on the subject, but, in order to get the work in its right perspective as regards the events of the times, he re-read Italian history for the period he was dealing with. Thus he enabled himself to gauge much more comprehensively the significance of the Bible Society's work in that country when viewed in relation to national happenings, public thought, and the attitude of mind of the Italian people.

PRELIMINARY READING HELPS YOU TO JUDGE THE WORTH OF YOUR INFORMATION

The writer of articles or books on general subjects (as distinct from fiction) must obviously do a good deal of research. And such reading for definite information has one value that is not always recognised by the amateur—it may let him know whether it is worth while to write the article at all!

Suppose, for example, that you have decided to write an article on "The Evolution of the Chimney-Pot." It is a foregone conclusion that you think you have a certain amount of exclusive information in your own head about chimney-pots, else there would be no call for you to write on this subject, since the public does not want articles containing nothing more than what has been published already.

You have collected some facts and information about chimney-pots, however, that you think are interesting and quite new. So far, good. Nevertheless, you will be wise to ascertain what has already been written on the subject; it may throw fresh light on your own gleanings.

First, you will probably look up the subject in a good encyclopædia—failing one of your own, consult one at a public library. If there is anything at all under this heading, it is just possible there may be cross-references that will be useful, and allusions to other works on the subject, which it would be well for you to get hold of if you can. Then you will also remember that Ruskin has written "A Chapter on Chimneys" in his *Poetry of Architecture*, with some delightful illustrations. And in the course of your explorations, some one may be able to direct you to other works on the subject, one book so often leads on to another. In this way you find you are absorbing quite a large amount of interesting information.

Yet presently you may make the very important discovery that what you were intending to say has already been said by others, and possibly said in a better and more authoritative manner than you could pretend to at present!

On the other hand, you may still consider that you have exclusive information; in that case do your best with it, and you will find your reading has given you a quickened interest and wider grasp of your subject. But if, in absolute honesty to yourself, you know you have nothing new to contribute to the information that has already been published, then do not attempt to offer your article for publication. Write it up, by all means, as a journalistic exercise for your own improvement; it will be helpful if you try how far you can seize, and sum up concisely, the important points that you came across in your various readings on the subject. *But don't attempt to pass off writing of this description as original matter.* Such methods never get you far.

Even though the Editor may not have studied chimney-pots in detail, and does not recognise that your "copy" is practically a *réchauffé* of other people's writings, some of the readers will know that it contains nothing original, and will lose no time in telling him so. There is one cheery thing about the public, no matter how busy it may be with its own personal affairs, and preoccupied with a war, or labour troubles, a Presidential election, or little trifles like that, it most faithfully keeps an Editor informed if anything printed in his pages does not meet with its entire approval!

And when an Editor finds he has been taken in with stale material, he naturally marks that contributor for future remembrance.

It is well to bear in mind that one of the most valuable assets in a writer's outfit is a reputation for absolute reliability. Smart practice, trickery, clever dodges, may get a hearing once, even twice—but they have no future whatever.

Let it become a recognised thing that whatever you offer for publication is new matter resulting from your own personal knowledge and investigation, and matter that is sure to interest a section of the general public; that you have verified every detail, and have ascertained, to the best of your ability, that the subject has not been dealt with in this particular way before;—then you are sure of a place somewhere in a mild atmosphere, if not actually in the sun!

Also, common sense should tell you that you are checking the development of your own ability, when you let yourself down (no less than the publisher) by trying to pass off other people's brain-work as your own. It doesn't pay either way.

READING FOR STYLE

Reading for the improvement of style will involve various types of literature. In order to know what you should read, you need to know in which particular direction you are weakest. In the main, however, I find that all amateurs require to cultivate—

1. A simple, clear, direct mode of expression.
2. Modern language and idiom—in the best sense.
3. A wide vocabulary.
4. An ear for musical, rhythmic sentences.

And equally they need to avoid—

1. Other people's mannerisms.
2. Long paragraphs and involved sentences.
3. Pedantry and a display of personal learning.
4. Hackneyed phrases.
5. Modern slang.

You may not be able to detect any corresponding weaknesses in your own writings; but, if you have had no special training in literary work, I can safely assure you they are there—some of them, possibly all of them! In any case, no particular harm will result if you assume that your writing will stand a little improvement under each of these headings, and start to work accordingly.

THE BEGINNER SELDOM USES SIMPLE, MODERN ENGLISH

In the first chapter I mentioned a lack of modernity in style as a frequent defect in the Mss. declined by publishers; unless you handled stories and articles all day long as an editor does you would never credit how widespread is the failing.

It is a curious fact that only a very small proportion of people can write as they actually speak; those who do so usually belong to the poorest of the uneducated classes, or they are experienced literary craftsmen.

The large majority of people are so self-conscious when they take pen in hand to write a story or an article, that they cannot be natural. They do not realise that they should write as ordinary human beings; they invariably feel they should write as famous authors; and they promptly drop the language they use as ordinary human beings in every-day life, and adopt an artificial, stilted style which they seem to think the correct thing for an author.

And this artificial phraseology is invariably archaic or Early Victorian, because the books people see labelled "good literature" or "the classics" are chiefly by dead-and-gone writers, who wrote in a style that sometimes sounds old-fashioned in these days, even though their English was excellent.

EVERY GENERATION SHOWS SPECIAL CHARACTERISTICS OF SPEECH

Our mode of speech and of writing in this twentieth century is not precisely that of Shakespeare or Milton, even though the fundamentals are the same. We live in a nervous, hurrying age, and our language is more nervous, more terse than it was even twenty years ago. We "speed up" our sentences, just as we "speed up" our stories and our articles. We have not time for lengthy introductions that arrive nowhere, and for ornate perorations that are superfluous. "Labour-saving" and "conservation of energy" are prominent watchwords of this present age, and are being applied to our language no less than to our work.

In order to get through all we must get through in a day (or, at any rate, all that we imagine we must get through!) it has become an unwritten law that the same thing must not be done twice over; more than this, we try to find the shortest cut to everywhere. As one result, we do not use two words where one will suffice; only the undisciplined, untrained mind employs a string of adjectives where one will convey the same idea, or repeats practically the same thing several times in succession.

Of course, all this curtailment can be—and often is—carried to excess, till only a few essential words are left in a sentence, and these are clipped of half their syllables; we find much of this in the newspapers and the periodicals of an inferior class. And it could be pushed so far, till at length we got to communicate with one another by nothing more than a series of grunts and snaps and snarls!

Modernity of Style is Desirable

But I am not dealing with the forms of speech used by the illiterate or the half-educated; I am referring to the language used by the most intelligent of the educated classes, and I want the amateur to remember that this is not necessarily the language of Shakespeare, even though the same words be employed. There is a subtle difference in the placement of words, in the turn of phrases, in the strength and even the meaning of words, in the shaping of sentences, and that difference is what, for want of a better word, I term "modernity," and it is a quality that the amateur requires to cultivate.

This lack of modernity is noticeable in amateurs of all types. It is a marked feature in the writings of teachers and those who have had a university education, or purely academic training; and equally it is conspicuous in the Mss. of the one who leads a very quiet, retired existence, or has a restricted view of life.

At first sight it may seem strange to the 'varsity girl, who considers herself the last word in modernity, that I classify her early literary attempts with those of a middle-aged invalid, let us say, who knows very little of the world at large.

But those who concentrate exclusively on one idea, or have their outlook narrowed to one particular groove—whether that groove be church-work, or housekeeping, or hockey, or reading for a degree—drop into an antiquated mode of expression, as a rule, the moment they start to write anything apart from a letter to an intimate. The rôle of author looms large before them. The mind instantly suggests the style of those authors they have been in the habit of reading—and more particularly those they would like other people to think they were in the habit of reading—the books that are accepted classics, and, consequently, must be beyond all question.

It matters not whether amateurs are shaping themselves according to Cowper and Miss Edgeworth, or striving to live up to the Elizabethan giants, they arrive at an old-fashioned style for which there is no more call in the world of to-day than there is for a crinoline or a Roman toga. And this, despite the greatness of their models.

Here are a few sentences taken at random from the pile of Mss. waiting attention here in my office:—

Instances of Antiquated Expressions

"Let us ponder awhile at the shrine of Nature." This is from an article on "A Country Walk," written by a High School teacher. Now, would she have said that, personally, either to a friend or to a class, if they were going out for a country walk? Of course not! You see at once how antiquated and stilted it is when you subject it to the test of natural, present-day requirements.

In another Ms. I read, "King Sol was seeking his couch in the west." Why not have said, "The sun was setting"?

"He was her senior by some two summers," writes a would-be novelist, in describing hero and heroine. Why "some" two summers, I wonder? And would it not be more straightforward to say, "He was two years older than she"?

"They were of respectable parentage, though poor and hard-working withal." Needless to say this occurs in a story of rustic life. Why is it that the amateur so often describes the cottager in this "poor but pious" strain?

"We saw ahead of us her home—to wit, a rose-grown, yellow-washed cottage." And a very pretty home it was, no doubt; but why spoil it by the introduction of "to wit"?

"He was indeed a meet lover for such an up-to-date girl." The word "meet" is not merely antiquated and unsuited to a story of present-day life; it seems particularly out of place when used in close connection with so modern a term as "up-to-date." The two expressions are centuries apart, and both should not have been included in the same sentence.

One Ms. says, "I would fain tell you of the devious ways in which the poor girl strove to earn an honest livelihood and keep penury at bay; but, alas! dear reader, space does not avail." On the whole, one is thankful that it didn't avail, all things considered!

In a letter accompanying another Ms. the author explains, "You won't find any slang in *my* writing. I revel in the rich sonority of the English language." That is all right; but some people confuse "rich sonority" with artificiality. A word may be richness itself if rightly applied, but if used in a wrong connection, or employed in an affected or unnatural manner, it will lose all its richness and become merely old-fashioned, or else absurd.

I have not the space to spare for further instances, but I notice one phrase that is curiously popular with the beginner, who frequently lets you know the name of some character in these words, "Mary Jones, for such was her name—" etc. I cannot understand what is the charm of that expression, "for such was her name"; but it is one of the amateurs' many stand-bys.

Common sense will tell you that the surest way to gain a good modern style is to read good modern stuff.

AND NOW FOR A REMEDY

Begin with a special study of the Editorials in the best type of newspapers. This is reading that I strongly advocate for the amateur in order to counteract archaic tendencies; though I wish emphatically to point out that by the "Leading Articles" I do not mean the average "Woman's Gossip," or whatever other name is given to the column of inanities that is devoted to feminine topics; for in some newspapers this is about as futile and feeble, and as badly written as it is possible for a newspaper column to be.

Unfortunately, the average person does not read the best part of the newspaper. He, and more particularly she, reads the headlines, skims the news, and runs the eye over anything that specially appeals, looks down the Births, Marriages and Deaths, and not much more. But this will not improve anyone's English.

Take a paper like the *Spectator*. Here you have modern journalistic writing at its best. Read the Leading Articles carefully each week. Read also the paragraphs summarising the news on the opening pages.

Read aloud, if you can; this will help to impress phrases and sentences on your mind. Observe how clear and concise and straightforward is the style. Of course, the articles will vary; they are not all written by the same pen; but those that follow immediately after the news paragraphs are always worth the student's attention. You will notice that the writer has something definite to say, and he says it plainly, in a way that is instantly understood. The words used will be to the point; there will be a good choice of language, yet never an unnecessary piling on of words. You may, or may not, agree with everything that is said; but that is not of paramount importance at the moment, as in this case you are reading in order to acquire a clear, easy style of writing rather than to gain special information. Nevertheless, you will be enlarging your mental outlook considerably.

In the same way, study the Editorials in any of the daily or weekly papers of high standing and reputation, avoiding the papers of the "sensational snippet" order. You will soon get to recognise whether the style is good or poor.

The *British Weekly* (London) is celebrated for its literary quality. It will be a gain if you read regularly the article on the front page, and "The Correspondence of Claudius Clear," which is a feature every week.

This is to start you on a course of reading that will give modernity to your style, and help to rid you of the antiquated expressions and mannerisms that are so noticeable in amateur work.

Mere "newspaper reading" may seem to you a disappointing beginning to the programme. "The newspaper is read by everybody every day," you may tell me, "and what has it done for their style?"

But I am not advocating that type of "newspaper reading." This isn't a question of reading some murder case, or imbibing the exhilarating information that some one met Mrs. Blank on Fifth Avenue the other day, and she looked sweet in a pale blue hat.

Leave all that part of the paper severely alone. Study the Editorials as you would study a book, since the writings of first-class journalists are excellent models for the amateur, a fact that is curiously overlooked by the student. Read a fixed amount each day, instead of relying on a haphazard picking up of a paper and a careless glance over its contents. Then, as a useful exercise, take the subject-matter of a paragraph, or an article, and see how *you* would have treated it; try if you can improve on it (after all, most things in this world can be improved upon if the right person does the improving). You will be surprised to find how interesting a study this will become in a very little while.

Do not misunderstand me: I am not advocating newspaper reading *in place* of classical works, but as a necessary and valuable addition to a writer's literary studies.

THE NEED FOR ENLARGING THE VOCABULARY

Equal in importance to the cultivation of a modern style in writing, is the necessity for having a wide selection of words at your command, and a keen sense of their value. Some people think the chief thing in writing is to have ideas in one's head. Ideas are essential, but they are not everything. Your brain may be crammed full of the most wonderful ideas, but they will be useless if they get no farther than your brain.

It is one thing to see things yourself, and quite another to be able to make an absent person see them.

It is one thing to receive impressions in your own mind from your surroundings, or as the product of imagination, and quite another to record those impressions in black and white.

Tens of thousands of people are conscious of vivid mental pictures, for one who is able to reproduce them in such a form that they become vivid pictures to others. And one reason for the inability of the majority to express their thoughts in writing is the paucity of their vocabulary, and their lack of the power to put words together in a convincing and accurate manner.

Girls often write to me, "I think such wonderful things in my brain; I'm sure I could write a book, if only people would give me a little encouragement," or, "if only I had time."

But if they had all the encouragement and all the time in the world, they could not transfer those wonderful thoughts from their brain to paper unless they had practice, the right words at their command, and the experience that comes from hard regular working at the subject.

What people do not realise is this: wonderful thoughts are surging through thousands of brains. They are fairly common *inside* people's heads; the difficulty is in getting them out of the head—as most of us soon find out when we start to write! I shall refer to this later on.

If you wish to write down your thoughts—no matter whether they are concerned with the emotions, or religion, or nature, or cookery—you must employ words; and the more subtle, or elevated, or complex the subject-matter of your thoughts, the greater need will there be for a wide choice of words, in order to express exactly the various grades and shades of meaning that will be involved.

If your vocabulary be small—*i.e.* if you only know the average words used by the average person—there is every chance that your writings will be flat and colourless, and no more interesting, or exciting, or instructive, or entertaining than the ordinary conversation of the average person.

Hence the necessity for enlarging your vocabulary, so that you have the utmost variety to choose from in the way of suitable words, expressive words, and beautiful words, (this last the modern amateur is apt to overlook).

The Average Person's Vocabulary is Meagre

The smallness of the vocabulary used by the average person to-day is partly due to the mass of feeble reading-matter with which the country was flooded in the years immediately preceding the War.

In addition to this, life had become very easy for the majority of folk in recent times; money was supposed to be life's sole requisite. Work of all kinds was "put out" as much as possible; we shirked physical labour; lessons were made as easy as they could be; games were played for us by professionals while we looked on; effort of every sort was distasteful to us. It has been said, that as a nation we were becoming flabby and inert, and were fast drifting into an exceedingly lazy, commonplace mental attitude. We boasted that we couldn't think (even though with many this was merely a pose); we seemed quite proud of ourselves when we proclaimed our indifference to all serious reading, and our inability to understand anything.

That pre-War period, given over to money-worship, not only curtailed our choice of words by its all-pervading tendency to mind-laziness, but it had its vulgarising effect upon our language, just as it had upon our dress, our mode of living, and our amusements.

The dull Monotony of English Slang

Not only did we cease to take the trouble to speak correctly, but we almost ceased to be lucid! We made one word—slang or otherwise—do duty in scores of places where its introduction was either senseless or idiotic, rather than exert our minds to find the correct word for each occasion. Many people appeared to think that the use of slang was not only "smart," but quite clever; whereas nothing more surely indicates a poor order of intelligence.

My chief objection to a constant use of slang is not because it is outside the pale of classical English, but because it is so ineffective and feeble.

As a rule, slang words and phrases are, in the main, pointless and weak, for the simple reason that we use one word for every occasion when it happens to be the craze; and before long it comes to means nothing at all, even if it chanced to mean anything at the start—which it seldom does.

Our grandmothers objected to their own set using slang on the ground that it was "unladylike." The modern girl smiles at the term. "Who desires to be 'lady-like'?" inquires the advanced young person of to-day. Yet our grandmothers were right fundamentally; with their generation, the word "lady" implied a woman of education, intelligence, and refinement. The user of slang is the person who lacks these qualifications; she has neither the wit nor the knowledge to employ a better and more expressive selection of words.

Slang indicates Ignorance

Slang indicates, not advanced ideas, but ignorance—any parrot can repeat an expression, it takes a clever person always to use the right word.

Many people who constantly employ any word that happens to be current, do not really know what they are saying, neither do they attach any weight to their words; they merely repeat some inanity, because they have not the brains to say anything more intelligent, or they are too indolent to use what brains they have.

Notice how a set of big schoolgirls will, at one time, use the word "putrid," let us say, and apply it to everything, from a broken shoe-lace to examinations. And women will call everything "dinkie," or "ducky," or something equally enlightening and artistic, working the word all day long until it is ousted by another senseless expression.

What power of comparison has a girl, such as one I met recently, who, in the course of ten minutes described a hat as "awf'ly niffy," a man as "awf'ly sweet," a mountain as "awf'ly rippin'," and another girl as an "awful cat"?

What does it all amount to, this perversion of legitimate words or introduction of meaningless ones? Nothing—actually nothing. That is the pity of it. If these "ornaments of conversation" enabled one to grasp a point better, to see things more clearly, or to arrive at a conclusion more rapidly, I, for one, would gladly welcome them, as I welcome anything that will save time and labour. But, unfortunately, they only tend to dwarf the intelligence and to lessen the value of our speech.

I have enlarged on the undesirability of slang, because many amateurs think it will give brilliance, or smartness, or up-to-date-ness to their work. But it doesn't. It obscures rather than brightens; it tends to monotony instead of smartness. The beginner will be wise to avoid it, unless it is required legitimately in recording the conversation of a slangy person.

SOME BOOKS THAT WILL ENLARGE YOUR VOCABULARY

To enlarge your selection of words, you must read books of the essay type rather than fiction, as these usually give the widest range of English. Two authors stand out above all others in this connection—Ruskin and R.L. Stevenson. Both men had an extraordinary instinct for the right word on all occasions—the word that expressed exactly the idea each wished to convey.

Read some of Stevenson's essays slowly and carefully. Don't gobble them! You want to impress the words, and the connection in which they are used, on your mind. It is an effort to most of us to read slowly in these hustling times; yet nothing but deliberate, careful reading will serve to teach the correct use of words and their approximate values. And I need not remind you to look up in a dictionary the meaning of any word that is new to you.

Ruskin's *Sesame and Lilies* you will have read many times, I hope; if not, get it as soon as ever you can. His *Poetry of Architecture* will make a useful study; also *Queen of the Air* and *Praeterita* (his own biography). His larger works, while containing innumerable passages of great beauty, are so often overweighted with technical details and principles of art (some quite out-of-date now) that they become tedious at times. Yet there is so much in all of his writings to enlarge your working-list of words, that you will benefit by reading any of his books.

Among present-day writers I particularly recommend Sir A. Quiller-Couch, Dr. Charles W. Eliot; Dr. A.C. Benson, Dr. Edmund Gosse, Coulson Kernahan, and

Augustine Birrell, whose volumes of essays will not only enlarge your vocabulary, but will prove particularly instructive in suggesting the right placing of words, and in giving you a correct feeling for their value.

Of course this does not exhaust the list of authors with commendable vocabularies; but it gives you something to start on.

IT IS THE VALUE OF A WORD, NOT ITS UNUSUALITY, THAT COUNTS

Notice that the writers I have suggested do not necessarily use extraordinary words, or uncommon words, or very long-syllabled words, or ponderous and learned words. One great charm of their writings lies in the fact that they invariably use the word that is exactly right, the word that conveys better than any other word the thought or sensation they wished to convey. Sometimes it is an unusual word; sometimes it is a familiar word used in an unfamiliar connection; but in most cases you feel that the word used could not have been bettered—it sums up precisely, and conveys to your mind instantly, the thought that was in the author's mind.

Many amateurs fall into the error of thinking that an uncommon word, or a long word, or a word with an imposing sound, gives style to their writings, and they despise the simple words, considering them common-place. I heard an old clergyman in a small country church explain to the congregation, in the course of a sermon, that the words "mixed multitude" meant "an heterogeneous conglomeration"; but I think his rustic audience understood the simple Bible words better than they did his explanatory notes.

I remember seeing an examination paper, wherein a student had paraphrased the line—

"The lowing herd wind slowly o'er the lea,"

as,

"The bellowing cattle are meandering tardily over the neglected, untilled meadow land."

This is an instance of the wrong word being used in nearly every case; and as a complete sentence it would have been difficult to construct anything, on the same lines, that conveyed less the feeling Gray wished to convey when he wrote the poem!

Good writing is not dependent upon long or ornate or unusual words; it is the outcome of a constant use of the right word—the word that best conveys the author's idea.

If there be a choice between a complex word and a simple word, use the simple one.

Remember that the object of writing is not the covering of so much blank paper, nor the stringing together of syllables; it is the transference from the author's brain to other people's brains of certain thoughts and situations and sensations. And the best writing is that which conveys, by the simplest and most direct means, the clearest reproduction of the author's ideas.

THE CHARM OF MUSICAL LANGUAGE

There is a very special and distinct charm about literature that is musical to the ear—words that are euphonious, phrases that are rhythmic, sentences that rise and fall with definite cadence.

Unfortunately, the twentieth century, so far, has been primarily concerned with the making of noise rather than music. Even before the War, we lived in a welter of hideous jarring sound, to which every single department of life has added its quota. Outdoors the vehicles honk and rattle and roar; in business life the clack and whirr of machinery drowns all else; in the home doors are banged, voices are raised to a raucous pitch, children are permitted to shout and clatter about at all times and seasons—indeed, it is the exception rather than the rule, nowadays, to find a quiet-mannered, well-ordered household.

When Strauss put together his sound monstrosities, which he misnamed music, he was only echoing the general noise-chaos that had taken possession of the universe, permeating art and literature no less than everyday life. The nightmares of the cubists and futurists were merely undisciplined blatancy and harshness rendered in colour instead of in sound, and were further demonstrations of the crudity to which a nation is bound to revert when it wilfully discards the finer things of the soul in a mad pursuit of money.

SOUND—REFINED AND OTHERWISE

The sounds produced by a people are invariably a direct indication of the degree of their refinement; the greater the blare and clamour attendant upon their doings, and the more harsh and uncultivated their speaking voices, the less their innate refinement.

Bearing all this in mind, it is easy to understand why so much of our modern literature became tainted with the same sound-harshness that had smitten life as a whole. Some writers would not take the trouble to be musical; some maintained that there was no necessity to be melodious; some regarded beauty of sound as synonymous with weakness; others—and these were in the majority—had lost all sense of word-music and the captivating quality of rhythm. And yet few things make a greater or a more general appeal to the reader.

THE DANGERS OF THE "ROUGH-HEWN" METHOD

There is no doubt but what the idea that rough, unpolished work stood for strength, while carefully-finished work implied weakness, was due to the fact that several of our great thinkers adopted the "rough-hewn" method. Such men as Carlyle and Browning were sometimes irritatingly discordant and unshapely in style—occasionally giving the idea, as a first impression, that their words were shovelled together irrespective of sound or sense.

Said the lesser lights, "This seems a very easy way to do it! And they are undoubtedly great men. Why shouldn't we do likewise? It must save a deal of trouble!"

But there is one difficulty that we lesser lights are always up against: whereas genius, in its own line, can do anything it likes, in any way it likes, and the result will be of value to the world, those of us who are not in the front rank of greatness cannot work regardless of all laws and traditions; or, if we do, our work is not worth much. It was not that Carlyle and Browning were permitted to write regardless of laws and traditions because they were great; certainly not. They were great because they could write regardless of laws and traditions, and yet write what was of value to the world. So few of us can do that.

Parenthetically, I am not saying that Browning was never musical; the lyrics in *Paracelsus*, for instance, are beautiful; but often he went to the other extreme.

It no more follows that beautiful language is weak, than that uncouth language is strong. The rough and often clumsy phraseology sometimes used by the two men I have named was their weakness; and the fact that the world was willing to accept the way they often said things, for the sake of what they had to say, is an immense tribute to the worth of their ideas.

To use Pleasing Language is Good Policy

There are invariably two ways of saying the same thing, and, all else being equal, it is more advantageous to say what we have to say in a pleasant rather than an unpleasant manner. We know the wisdom of this in everyday life; equally it is the best policy in writing.

I could name books that are moderately thin in subject-matter and yet have had a large sale, and this, primarily, because of the charm of their style and the music of their language.

While there should be ideas behind all that is written, if those ideas are presented in language that captivates the ear, the book has a double chance, since it will appeal through two channels instead of only one—the ear as well as the mind.

It must never be forgotten that the object of our reading is sometimes—very often, indeed—recreation and recuperation. We are not always seeking information; the mind is not always equal to profound or involved thought; but it is always susceptible to beauty and harmony (or it should be, if we keep it in a healthy condition, and do not damage it with injurious mental food). And whether we are seeking information or recreation, there is a great fascination in reading matter that has rhythm, melody, and balance in its sentences.

I consider that the power to write on these lines is very largely a matter of training. Though, obviously, some ears are more keenly alive than others to the comparative values of sound, and some are born with a certain instinct for good expression, there is no doubt but what practice will do much to induce a graceful, melodious style of writing, and study will help us to detect these qualities in the works of others.

WRITE VERSE IF YOU WANT TO WRITE GOOD PROSE

With regard to training: I strongly advise those who aim for a good prose style to practise writing verse. When you start, you will probably find that your early attempts are nothing more than a series of lines with jingling rhymes at stated intervals.

Nevertheless, even such productions as these are of definite use in your training. You have had to find words that rhymed. You have had to compress your ideas within a set limit; this in itself is a check on the long-winded wandering tendencies of the amateur. You have had to consider the respective weight of syllables—which is worth an accent, and which is not, and so on. In short, you have had to give some discriminating thought to what you were writing, and how you were writing it, and that is what the beginner so seldom does. He more often sits down and goes on and on and on—words, words, words—with no feeling for their respective values, or the proportion of the sentences and incidents as a whole.

Viscount Morley, in his *Recollections*, writes: "At Cheltenham College, I tried my hand at a prize poem on Cassandra; it did not come near the prize, and I was left with the master's singular consolation, for an aspiring poet, that my verse showed many of the elements of a sound prose style."

But the master's consolation was not so singular after all. It is quite possible for one to write verse that may be excellent training for prose writing, and yet that is not poetry in the most exclusive sense of the word.

READ POETRY ALOUD TO CULTIVATE A SENSE OF MUSICAL LANGUAGE

In addition to writing verse, I urge all students who wish to cultivate a sense of music in their writing to read good poetry, and, whenever possible, to read it aloud.

When reading aloud, the ear helps as well as the eye; whereas, when reading silently, the eye is apt to run on faster than the ear is able—mentally—to take in the sounds; and you are bound to miss some of the finer shades of movement and melody. When you say the words aloud, the sound and the beat of the syllables are more likely to be impressed upon your mind.

You cannot do better than Tennyson to begin with—one of the most musical of our poets. Read "The Lotos-Eaters," the lyrics in "The Princess," "The Lady of Shallott," "Come into the Garden, Maud." In "The Idylls," and "In Memoriam," are many exquisite passages. Read "Guinevere," and "The Passing of Arthur," for example, noting the lines that are conspicuous for their charm of wording, or balance, or sound.

Turning to other writers: I select a few instances at random, and am only naming well-known poems that are within the reach of most students:—

Christina Rossetti: The chant of the mourners, at the end of "The Prince's Progress," beginning "Too late for love," is worth reading many times.

Jean Ingelow has, in a marked degree, a musical quality in her verse which compensates in some measure for its slightness. Her habit of repeating a word often gives a lilt and a cadence to her lines that is very pleasing, as for instance in "Echo and the Ferry," and "Songs of Seven." As an example by another poet, this repetition of a word is used with delightful effect in "Sherwood," by Alfred Noyes.

Other poems you might read are: "The Forsaken Merman," Matthew Arnold; "The Cloud," Shelley; "Kubla Khan," Coleridge; "The Burial of Moses," Mrs. Alexander; and "The Recessional," Kipling. "The Forest of Wild Thyme," Alfred Noyes, contains much in the way of music.

After you have studied these—and they will give you a good start—search for yourself. To make your own discoveries in literature is a valuable part of your training.

ANTHOLOGIES ARE VALUABLE TEXT-BOOKS

The student will find it very helpful to have at hand one or two small volumes of selected poems by various authors. Such anthologies often give, in a compact form, some of the choicest of the writers' verses; and this saves the novice's time in wading through some work that may be indifferent in search of the best. Moreover, a little volume can be slipped into the pocket, and will provide reading for odd moments.

Do not content yourself with a mere reading of the poems. Try to decide wherein lies the charm (or the reverse) of each. Explain, if you can, why, for instance, the following, by Swinburne:—

> "Yea, surely the sea like a harper laid hand on the shore as a lyre,"

appeals to one more than Longfellow's lines:—

> "The night is calm and cloudless,
> And still as still can be,
> And the stars come forth to listen
> To the music of the sea."

Compare poems by various writers dealing with somewhat similar themes; note wherein the difference lies both in thought and workmanship. Mrs. Browning's "Sonnets from the Portuguese" could be studied side by side with Christina Rossetti's "Monna Innominata"; Longfellow's "The Herons of Elmwood" with Bryant's "Lines to a Waterfowl"; Christina Rossetti's "The Prince's Progress" with Tennyson's "The Day Dream."

Such exercises will enlarge your ideas as well as your vocabulary; they will help to give you facility in expressing yourself, and also that genuine polish which is the result of close familiarity with good writing.

ANALYSING AN AUTHOR'S METHODS

It is not possible to suggest any definite course of reading for the study of technique (or methods of authorship). The ground is too wide to be covered by any prescribed set of books.

In order to understand, even a little bit, "how the author does it," you need to study each book separately, as you read it—deciding, if you can, what was the author's central idea in writing it; disentangling the essential framework of the story from the less important accessories; analysing the plot; assigning to the various characters their degree of importance; accounting for the introduction of minor episodes; noting how the author has obtained a fair proportion of light and shade, and secured sufficient contrast to ensure a well-balanced story; and how all the main happenings combine to carry one forward, slowly it may be, but surely, to the climax the author has in view.

These are a few of the points you should observe. Now look at them in detail, and at the same time apply them to your own work.

ONE CENTRAL IDEA SHOULD UNDERLIE EVERY STORY

Every author of any standing has one central idea at the back of his mind when he sets out to write a novel; this is the pivot on which the plot turns—it may be called the keynote of the book, Sometimes the author's "idea" is obvious or avowed, as in the case of much of Dickens's works, and *Uncle Tom's Cabin*. Sometimes it is so deftly concealed that you may not realise a book is giving expression to any one special idea, so absorbing is the general interest.

One great advantage of this keynote is the way it gives cohesion to a story as a whole, a motive for the plot, a bed-rock reason for the story's existence.

The central idea which is invariably behind a well-written story must not be confused with the "moral" that adorned all the praiseworthy books of our grandmothers' day. The idea may be a very demoralising one, and anything but a wholesome pill administered in a little jam, as was the "moral" of by-gone story-books. But the point I want you to notice is this: every author who is an experienced worker starts out with a definite object in mind—good or bad, or merely dull, as the case may be; he does not sit down and write haphazard incidents with nothing more in view than the stringing together of conversations and happenings that arrive nowhere, and illustrate nothing in particular, and reach no climax other than a wedding.

A WEDDING NEED NOT BE THE CHIEF AIM OF A NOVEL

Possibly it will come as a surprise to many amateurs when I tell them that the inevitable uniting of the lovers (or their disuniting, as the case may be) in the last chapter, is not necessarily the chief object of an experienced writer; often it is merely incidental.

The average beginner—more especially the feminine beginner—has but one aim when she embarks on fiction, viz., the marrying of her hero and heroine. That the wedding bells ringing on the last page may be an episode of secondary importance, so far as a book is concerned, seldom occurs to her. The result is the monotonous character of thousands of the Mss. offered for publication; and the weary reams of paper that are covered with pointless, backboneless fiction, that amounts, all told, to nothing more than the engagement (or the estrangement) of two colourless, nondescript individuals!

THE IDEAS BEHIND BOOKS ARE AS VARIED AS HUMAN NATURE

Sometimes the author aims to show you either the inhabitants and manners and customs and scenery of some definite locality! or one particular class of society; or the virtues or failings of an individual type; or the beauty of an abstract virtue; or the pitiful side of poverty; or vice decorated with gloss and glamour.

But whatever the idea may be, one of some sort lies behind every novel of recognised standing.

Begin your study of a book, therefore, by looking for its central idea; then observe how this permeates the whole, and how the author utilises his characters and his incidents to demonstrate the idea.

Some writers explain themselves in the title they give to a book. *The Egoist* tells you at once what to expect. But whether the motif of a book be obvious or not at first apparent, it is important so far as the staying quality of a story is concerned. And it is not until you have studied standard authors, with this particular matter in mind, that you realise how much more important it is that a book should have a keynote, than that the hero should be handsome, or that the heroine should be dressed in some soft clinging material that suits her surpassing loveliness to perfection.

LOOK FOR THE FRAMEWORK OF THE STORY

Having decided what is the central idea behind the book you are studying (I am not suggesting any particular book; choose any work of recognised merit by a dead or a modern writer and it will serve), next try to find the framework of the story—the plot if you like, though the framework is not always the plot.

Each complete story is composed of an essential skeleton, with a certain amount of secondary matter added to it to take away from its bareness. It is well to notice that with the greatest writers the framework is usually something fairly solid and substantial that will stand the addition of other matter; and it often deals with some great human truth that is world-old. It is not much good to have a framework composed of trivialities.

But suppose the framework be something like this—

Worthy John Jones becomes engaged to good Mary Smith; they quarrel, and become disengaged. J. J. falls a temporary prey to the sirenical wiles of Elsienoria Brown; M. S. lends a temporary ear to the insidious suggestions of Adolphus Robinson. Elsienoria Brown inadvertently listens to the innocent prattle of a little orphan child, and forthwith mends her wicked ways and dies of consumption; Adolphus Robinson is condemned to penal servitude for life after absconding with the Smith family plate.

J. J. and M. S. are finally restored to each other through the kind offices of the same innocent orphan child.

It may take you a little thought and time to detach this framework from the author's wealth of additional incidents or secondary matter.

There may be talk about the lovely old Tudor mansion, Mary's home; the life history of each of Mary's ancestors, whose portraits hang in the long gallery; the eccentricities of Mary's grandfather; the Spartan temperament of Mary's mother, with details about the perfection of her servants, and the thoroughness of her spring-cleaning activities; digressions as to non-successful aspirants for Mary's hand prior to the advent of John; Mary's work among the poor; Mary's love of Nature, and her exquisite taste in garden planning; Mary's patience with a gouty father; the sordid history of the late parents of the prattling orphan child whom Mary recently adopted; Mary's stay in Cairo (after the quarrel), and her meeting there with Adolphus; details of Cairo natives; measurements of the pyramids; a nocturne on moonlight over the desert; a dissertation on flies; prices and descriptions of bazaar curios; sidelights on hotel visitors, their tongues, their flirtations, and their fancy-work—

And much more concerning Mary.

Then there will be Elsienoria; her stage career; her intrigues; her eyes; her interest in bull-terriers and bridge; a descriptive catalogue of her jewels, and the furnishings of her palatial yacht; and a vignette of her poor old mother taking in washing in Milwaukee.

In like manner there will be copious data concerning John, and ditto concerning Adolphus, with all sorts of entanglements to be straightened out, and a legion of simple happenings that lead to confusions.

It is from a mass of incidents such as these that you will have to eliminate the framework, the part that cannot be dispensed with without the rest falling to pieces. Practice in analysing stories will soon make the framework of each clear to you.

ASSESS THE VALUE OF EACH CHARACTER IN THE STORY

The characters should be studied individually, in order to find out why the author brought them on the scene; what position each occupies in relation to the whole; who are the most important folk, and who are brought in merely to render some useful but unimportant service to the story.

Then note how the author keeps the circumstances that surround each character directly proportionate to his or her place in the story. The great deeds are invariably performed by the hero—not by some odd man who appears only in one chapter and is never heard of again. The most striking personality is never assigned to some woman who only has a minor part given her, and who vanishes in the course of a dozen pages, with no further explanation.

In this way assess the value of each character to the story as a whole.

Next study the matter that seems non-essential to you, and decide, if you can, why each episode was introduced.

The Use of Secondary Matter

At first glance you may think that much of it could be done without, and would make no difference whatever to the story, beyond shortening it, if it were omitted altogether.

This is perfectly true of poor work. The unskilled writer will pad out a Ms. with all manner of stuff that has no direct bearing on the plot. There will be conversations that reveal nothing, that throw no lights on the characteristics or the motives of anybody, and are obviously introduced merely to fill up a few pages. There will be incidents that in no way affect the movement of the story, that add no particular excitement or interest, and carry you no nearer to the climax than you were in the previous chapter.

But the good craftsman wastes no space on unnecessary talk, even though certain scenes and episodes may be of less importance than others. He knows that secondary matter, such as descriptive passages, dialogues, interludes and digressions are necessary in order to "dress" the framework and give it something more than bare bones; they are also needed to give variety and balance to a book. Some incidents that may not appear to be vital to the story, are introduced to break what would otherwise have been a monotonous series of events; or they are put in for the purpose of giving brightness and a picturesque element as a contrast to some sorrowful or gloomy occurrence.

Minor Details can be made to serve Two Purposes

If the book be written by a master, each character, each conversation, each incident, each descriptive passage, each soliloquy is introduced for a specific purpose; nothing is haphazard, nothing is merely a fill-up.

Moreover, the expert novelist is not content to put his secondary matter to one minor use only; he frequently makes it contribute something to the main issues of the story—and in this case it serves a double purpose.

For instance, take the imaginary story I sketched out just now. Let us suppose that, half-way through the story, there occurs a stormy chapter, in which John and Mary quarrel and part in a scene that is red-hot with temper and emotion. It will be desirable to secure a decided contrast in the next chapter, to give every one—readers as well as lovers—time to cool down a little; besides, you do not follow one emotional scene with another that is equally overwrought, or they weaken each other. The author would, therefore, aim for something entirely different in the chapter following the one that ended with John violently slamming the hall door, and Mary drowning the best drawing-room cushion in tears.

We will assume that the author transports Mary to Cairo for change of air; and, in order to restore the atmosphere to normal, he decides on an interlude, entitled "Moonlight Over the Desert"; this will serve as a soothing contrast to the preceding upset.

But he will not necessarily describe the moonlight himself. If he makes Mary describe it in a letter to a friend, or to her father who remained at home, he will be killing two birds with one stone; he will be administering a pleasant sedative, after the turmoil of the lovers' quarrel; also he will be showing you how Mary's temperament responds to the beauties of Nature, and how appreciative she is of all that is good and pure and lovely. In this way he will be helping you to understand Mary better, and thus the "Moonlight Over the Desert" chapter will be contributing definitely to the main trend of the book.

Then, again, the author may wish to bring the reader back to the everyday happenings in a light and whimsical manner, and he may give you a scene showing the various ladies who are staying at the same hotel with Mary in Cairo, retailing their conversation, with the usual oddities and humours and irresponsibilities that are to be found in the small-talk of a mixed collection of women at an hotel. In this way he can introduce brightness and a light touch among more sombre chapters. But in all probability he will make the conversation serve a second purpose; Mary may, on this occasion, hear the name of Adolphus Robinson for the first time, little realising that he is to play an important part in her life later on; or an American visitor may chance to give details of her old charwoman in Milwaukee, Elsienoria's mother, little knowing that Elsienoria is the evil star in Mary's horizon, etc.

These are indications of the way an experienced author can make every incident in the story dovetail with something else, as well as serve an "atmospheric" purpose, i.e., to change the air from grave to gay, or from mirth to tragedy. He never writes merely for the sake of covering paper, or bridging time; whereas the amateur only too often introduces digressions and irrelevant matter with very little reason or apparent connection, apart from a desire to cover paper, or, perhaps, because the episode came into his mind at that moment, and he thought it was interesting in itself, or that it would help to lengthen the story.

NEVER LOSE SIGHT OF THE CLIMAX

Notice, too, how the clever author keeps his eye on the climax; how ingeniously he will make everything lead towards that climax; and how he puts on pace as he gets nearer and nearer the goal, instead of hurrying on events at a terrific rate at the beginning, then getting suddenly becalmed part-way through, and making the tragedy painfully long-drawn-out at the end—as is the method of many amateurs!

THE MAIN RULES APPLY TO ALL STORIES, IRRESPECTIVE OF LENGTH

You may tell me that all this does not apply to you personally, as you are not so ambitious as to try your hand at a book; you only write short stories.

The same rules apply to all stories, whether 3,000 or 100,000 words in length, the difference being that with a short story greater condensation is necessary. Instead of devoting a chapter to some contrasting episode, you would give a paragraph to it; and instead of having a dozen or so secondary characters, you would be content with only two or three besides the hero and heroine, and this in itself would reduce your number of minor episodes and your descriptive matter.

Whatever the length of your story, it is well to remember that there should be one main idea at the back of all (apart from the wedding); also a framework, to which is added a certain amount of secondary matter that is well-balanced and introduced with a definite object in view; the characters must bear a fixed relation to the whole; and there must be a climax, concealed from the reader, so far as possible, till the last moment, but ever-present in the writer's mind as the goal towards which every incident, indeed every paragraph, in the story trends.

You will find it very useful to study the short stories of Rudyard Kipling, Sir James Barrie, and Mrs. Flora Annie Steel.

The Necessity for Careful Planning

Studying fiction in this way is exceedingly interesting, and wonderfully instructive. Obviously every author has his own individual methods, and no two work in exactly the same way. But if you examine these main features, which are common to most, you begin to realise something of the careful planning and forethought that go to the making of a story that is to grip its readers, and live beyond its first publication flush.

Perhaps you may be inclined to think that the bestowal of such minute care on the details of a book would tend to make it artificial and stilted; there are those who argue that the rough, slap-dash style is the only method by which we can catch the fine frenzy of genius in its unadulterated form! But all Art calls for attention to detail; anything that is to last must be the product of painstaking thought. Life itself is a mass of detail carefully planned by the Master-Mind. If you study your own life, you will be amazed to find, as you look back upon the past, how every happening seems to be part of a wonderful mosaic, that nothing really stands quite alone with no bearing whatever on after events.

That the slap-dash method is much easier than the careful, thoughtful working-out of a story, I admit. But it does not wear—why? because there is really no body in the work; it is all on the surface, and therefore quickly evaporates. That which costs you next to nothing to produce, will result in next to nothing.

Of course, you can elaborate your work, and add a multitude of details all apparently bearing on the story, till the readers (and also the main features of the story) are lost in a mass of small-talk and unimportant events. But the secret of all good art is to know what to take and what to leave; and the genius of a writer is evidenced in the way he knows just what incidents to put down in order to gain the object he has in view, and what to omit as redundant, or unnecessary to the direct working out of his theme.

THE APPLICATION

I am not analysing any novel to give you concrete examples of the points I have named. My object in writing these chapters is not so much to set down facts for you to memorise, as to help you to find out things for yourself.

Our own discoveries are among the few things of life that we manage to remember.

Having dissected a novel, and made notes on the way it was constructed, turn to your own work (whether a long or a short story), and see what you have to show in the way of a main idea, a good framework, a purpose for each character, a reason for each incident, well-balanced secondary matter, with a steady *crescendo* and *accelerando* leading to a good climax.

I need not point out the application. It is for you to make your own stories profit by your study of the methods of the great writers.

Part Four

Points a Writer Ought to Note

Beautiful and striking thoughts are a common everyday occurrence; the uncommon occurrence is to find the person who can reduce those thoughts to writing in such a manner as to convey, exactly to another mind the ideas that were in his own.

Practice Precedes Publication

When you sit down pen in hand with the intention of writing something—Write!

This may seem unnecessary advice to lead off with; but it is surprising how much time one can spend in not writing, when one is supposed to be engaged in literary work (no one knows this better than I do). It is so easy to gaze out of the window in pleasant meditation, letting the thoughts wander about in a half-awake, half-dreaming state of mind.

Girls often sit and think all kinds of romantic things, weaving one strand of thought with another, letting the mind run on indefinitely into space and roam about aimlessly among pleasant sensations. Such girls sometimes think this an indication that they have the ability to write a novel; whereas it is doubtful whether they could draft a possible plot for the simplest of stories; their brain is not sufficiently disciplined to consecutive thought.

Others are possessed of high, noble impulses; or they feel a sudden overwhelming sense of the beautiful in life; or a desire to attain to some lofty ideal; and forthwith they conclude this indicates a poetic gift of unusual calibre. All such experiences are good, they are also plentiful (fortunately, for the uplifting of human nature); but they do not imply the ability to write good poetry, even though they prove exceedingly useful to a poet.

Beautiful Thoughts do not Guarantee Beautiful Writing

Most beginners think that the main essential for a writer is a fair-sized stock of beautiful or striking thoughts; but it is quite as important to know how to write down those thoughts. As a matter of fact, beautiful and striking thoughts are of common, everyday occurrence; the uncommon occurrence is to find the person who can reduce those thoughts to writing in such a manner as to convey, exactly, to another mind the ideas that were in his own.

"But how ought I to start with writing?" the novice sometimes asks. "There seems so much to say, yet it is difficult to know where to begin."

When a student commences the study of Art he does not begin with the painting of some big, involved subject, such as "A Scene from Hamlet." He spends some years working at little bits and making studies. He practises on a profile, or a hand, or the branches of a tree; he will sketch and re-sketch a child's head, or one figure; he will work away at a few rose-petals or an apple—always endeavouring to render small pieces of work well, rather than large pieces indifferently.

When a great artist starts work on an Academy picture, he does not commence at one side of the canvas and work right across to the other side till the picture is finished. He does not necessarily begin his masterpiece by painting on the canvas at all. As a rule, he makes a rough-out of his idea (more than one, very often), merely blocking in the figures, arranging and re-arranging the position of the main items, then assigning the details to their proper places, till he gets all properly balanced, and to his liking.

Then he dissects the picture-that-is-to-be, making separate studies of the figures, sometimes making several drawings of an arm, or a piece of drapery, or a bit of foreground, expending infinite care and work on fragments, and making dozens of sketches before a stroke is put on the canvas itself.

Thus you see both the novice and the master specialise on detail before they tackle a piece of work as a whole.

Some of the "studies" made by famous artists for their important pictures are positive gems, and help us to understand something of the immense amount of thought and preparation that go to the making of any work of art that is to live.

The student who is training for authorship must work on the same lines. All too often the amateur starts by putting down the first sentence of a story or an article, and then writes straight on to the very end, without any preliminary rough-out or separate study of detail; and the result is a shapeless mass of words, lacking balance and variety, and either without any climax, or with two or three too many.

"It simply Came!"

When offering a Ms. for publication, the writer will often tell me—as though it were something to be proud of—"I merely sat down, and without any previous thought, wrote the whole of this story from beginning to end. It simply came."

One can only reply: "It reads like it!"

I have before me a letter and Ms. from a would-be contributor, who writes: "I just dashed this off as it first came into my head. I do so love scribbling, and I simply can't help jotting things down when the fit takes me."

This is very well to a limited extent. There are times when all authors just dash things off when the fit takes them; but, if they have any sense (and no one succeeds as a writer if they have not) they do not regard the dashed-off scribble as the final product, and rush with it to a publisher. Much ability may be evidenced in a hurried "jot-down" of this type; and if written by a master hand, it may be useful as an object lesson, showing how a clever author makes his preliminary studies; but as a finished piece of work it is of little value, for the simple reason that it is not finished.

Of course, the greater the writer the less revision will his dashed-off-scribble need, because experience and practice have taught him to know almost by instinct what to put down and what to omit. Nevertheless, he is certain to go over it again, making alterations and additions, before sending it out to the reading public.

Before you can hope to write anything worth publication (much less worth payment), you will require considerable practice in actual writing.

Directly a beginner puts on paper a little study in observation, or collects some facts from various already-published books, or induces twelve or sixteen lines of equal lengths to rhyme alternately (rhymes sometimes omitted, however, in which case the lines are styled "blank verse"), that beginner invariably sends along the Ms. to an editor, and is surprised, or grieved—according to temperament—when it is not accepted.

Few would-be authors realise that what may be good as a study or an exercise, is not necessarily of the slightest use to the general public. And, after all, the final test of our work is its use to the public. If the public will not take it, it may just as well remain unwritten (unless we are willing to regard it as practice only), for it is certain our acquaintances will not listen while we read our "declined" Mss. aloud to them!

"But why shouldn't the public buy my first attempt?" some one will ask.

WHY "FIRST ATTEMPTS" HAVE RARELY ANY MARKET VALUE

The public seldom is willing to pay some one else for what it can do quite as well itself. And most people have made first attempts at writing. Rare indeed is the person who has not laboured out an essay, or dreamed a wonderful love story, or put together a few verses. In the main, all first attempts bear a strong family likeness one to the other, and though the general public may not stop to analyse its own motives, the truth is, it will not buy immature work as a rule, because it feels it can produce writing equally immature.

For this reason (among other things) first attempts have rarely any market value—unless you have been dead at least fifty years and have acquired fame in the interval!

Of course there is always the remote chance that a genius may arise, whose first attempt eclipses everything else on the market; but as I have said before, we need not worry about that exceptional person, since some one has estimated that not more than two are born in any generation. And even these two have to be divided between a number of arts and sciences; they are not devoted exclusively to literature!

The average writer whose books have made his name famous, had to write much by way of practice, before any of it found a paying market. And we humbler folk must not be above doing likewise.

Begin to train yourself in writing by making studies, in words, just as the art student makes them in line or wash. Make studies of character, of scenery, of temperament, of dialogue—of anything that comes to your notice and interests you.

To make a character study of someone you know intimately, or with whom you are in daily contact, is a useful exercise—but I don't advise you to read it to them afterwards, that is if you feel you have been quite frank in your writing, and you value their friendship!

Aim to make each study a little word-picture, embodying some idea, or re-producing some trait, or conversation, or incident. But do not be in too great a hurry to embark on a lengthy or involved piece of work.

THE STYLE OF WRITING SHOULD VARY ACCORDING TO THE SUBJECT-MATTER

Practise various styles of writing—serious, conversational, gay, didactic, colloquial, etc.; and see that the style corresponds with your subject-matter.

Watch good authors with this latter point in view. For example, the style of writing in Kipling's "Barrack Room Ballads" is not the style he used when writing "The Recessional."

Often several styles of writing are necessary in one story, if we are introducing contrasts in characters or in scenes. And though we may think that one style is peculiarly our own, it is most desirable that we should write just as readily in any style. This gives variety and colour to our work; also it reduces the risk of our acquiring mannerisms, which are generally tiresome to other people, though we are blandly unconscious of them ourselves.

But be sure that you do not appear to force an effect; do not make an effort to be light-hearted, for instance, or overdo the sombre tone one would use at a funeral. Sincerity should underlie all your writings; they should carry the conviction with them that what you say happened, actually *did* happen, and was not invented by you merely to heighten the gaiety or deepen the gloom, as the case may be.

In order to make your style sincere and convincing, you must study life itself, not take your models from other people's books. If you are to write in a joyous style that will infect others with your cheeriness, you must enjoy much of life (if not all of it) yourself, and be able to enter into other people's enjoyment. If you are to make your readers feel the grief that surrounded the funeral of which you write in your story, you must have shared in sorrow and sympathised with others in theirs.

Once you enter into the very spirit of each happening, you will find your style will soon shape itself according to the situation. You will use the right words and expressions just as you would were you facing the situation in real life, without having to stop to think out what is best suited to the occasion.

But the beginner has to learn to be natural when writing; that is one of his hardest tasks, I often think; and he sometimes needs considerable practice before he acquires the power to write exactly as he thinks and speaks, and convey precisely what he himself feels. Therefore practise your pen particularly in this direction if you find it an effort to be natural on paper.

THE NEED FOR CONDENSATION

All beginners need to practise condensation; our tendency while we are inexperienced is to be diffuse, and to over-load our subject with unimportant explanations or irrelevant side-issues.

It will help you if, after a finished piece of writing has been put aside for a few days, you go over it with a fresh mind, and delete everything—single words or whole sentences—that can be omitted without lessening the force or the picturesque quality of your writing, or blurring your meaning.

For example:—If the hero's grandfather has no bearing on the development of the story (and you are not seeking to prove hereditary tendencies), spare us his biography.

Do not tell the reader, "It is impossible to describe the scene," if you straightway proceed to describe it.

It is waste of space to write, "It was a dull, gloomy, cheerless November day"; one takes it for granted that a gloomy November day is dull, likewise cheerless.

If the colour of the heroine's eyes and the tint of her hair are immaterial to her career, omit such hackneyed data. Of course these matters may be important—if the lady is the villainess, for instance. I have noticed that it seems essential the wicked female should have red hair and green eyes, while the angel has violet (or grey) eyes, with long sweeping lashes—in novels, at any rate. I cannot be so certain about real life, for I have never met an out-and-out villainess in the flesh; though I have known several really nice girls, who were a joy to their aged and decrepit parents, and who married the right man into the bargain—and all this on mere mouse-coloured hair, nondescript eyebrows, and complexions verging on sallow!

If, after consideration, you are bound to admit that it will make no difference to the working out of the story, nor to its general interest, if you omit some such trivial description, or a word or a phrase, take it out; its deletion will probably improve the Ms. In such a matter, however, it is very difficult for us to judge our own work.

The Quest of the Right Word

As a useful exercise in the art of condensation, practise describing incidents as forcefully as you can, using the fewest possible sentences. This will also train you to select the word that best describes your idea. You will soon realise that the one right word (and there is always one right word for every occasion) carries more conviction with it than half-a-dozen words when neither is exactly "it."

The able writer is not the one who uses many words, but he who invariably uses the exact word.

It is safe to say that, as a general rule, the more you increase your adjectives, and qualifying or explanatory phrases, the more you decrease the strength and vividness of your writing.

Making Plots

The student should practise sketching out plots. This is a very fascinating occupation, and all seems to go easily here—until you examine them! Then you may be less elated.

When you have completed the plot to your own satisfaction, look at it carefully in order to discover if you have, by any chance, used an idea or a theme that has been used by some one else before you. This is a painful process, for, as a rule, one's most admired plot crumbles to nothing under this test! If you are quite honest about it, you will be obliged to confess—until you have had a fair amount of practice—that your plots are nothing more than other people's plots re-shuffled.

Do not delude yourself by saying that you will "treat it differently." Perhaps you will; but you will stand more chance of success if you determine to get a new plot that has not been used before, and treat *that* differently.

The lack of any new idea or originality in the plot is the cause of thousands of Mss. being turned down each year. Many amateurs seem to think that the plot is of next to no importance, whereas it is the foundation upon which you raise the superstructure; if there is no strength in the foundation, the upper part is likely to be tottery.

LEARNING AND CLEVERNESS MUST NOT BE OBTRUSIVE

Until you start to scheme out plots, you have no idea how much there can be (but often is not!) in this part of an author's business.

Do not regard your writing as a medium for the exhibition of your own cleverness. Never try to show off your own learning or to impress the reader with your own brilliancy.

Early amateur efforts often bristle with quotations, foreign words, stilted phrases, pedantic remarks, or references to classical personages. The reason for this is clear; when the amateur writes he invariably sees himself as the chief object of interest in the foreground, rather than his subject-matter. Almost unconsciously the back of his mind is filled with the thought, "What will the public think of me when they read this?" Consequently he does all in his power to impress the public, and his relations and friends (and by no means forgetting his enemies) with his attainments and unusual knowledge.

We are all of us like this when we start. But as we gain experience—not merely experience in writing, but that wide experience of the world and human nature, which is such a valuable asset to the writer—we come to realise that the public pay very little heed to a writer personally (until he or she becomes over-poweringly famous); it is the subject-matter of a book that they trouble about, and the way that subject-matter is treated. Readers do not care in the least if an author can read Hafiz in the original (unless he is actually writing about Persian poetry, of course); but they do care if he has written a bright, absorbing story that holds their interest from first to last, or a helpful illuminating article on some topic that appeals to them. Therefore, why make a special opportunity to drag in Hafiz, or some one equally irrelevant, when he is but vaguely related to the subject in hand, or possibly is quite superfluous?

Do not think I mean by this that a knowledge of languages and the classics is immaterial or unnecessary for the writer. Quite the reverse. The more knowledge we acquire of everything worth knowing (and standard literature is the great storehouse of knowledge) the better equipped we are for work, and the greater our chance of success.

The Well-Informed Man does not use his Learning for Show Purposes

But remember this: the really well-informed man does not use his learning for show purposes. Knowledge should not be employed for superficial ornamentation. It must be so woven into the strands of our everyday life, that it becomes as much a part of us as the food we eat and the air we breathe. Our reading should not be made to advertise our intellectual standing.

We do not read Plato and Shakespeare and Dante that we may be able to quote them, and thus let others know we are familiar with them. We read them in order to get a wider outlook on life; to see things from more than one point of view; to look into minds that are bigger than our own; to learn great facts and problems of life that might not otherwise come our way, yet are necessary for us to know, if we are to see human nature in right perspective. In short, we study great authors in order to arrive at a better understanding of our neighbour; some take us farther than this, and help us to a better understanding of God and His Universe. If we are reading the classics with any lesser aim, we are missing a great deal.

The knowledge we absorb from such reading should work out to something far greater than a few quotations! It should affect our thoughts and our life itself (which obviously includes our writing), because it has helped us to clearer, altogether larger ideas of this world of ours and the people who are in it.

Such knowledge will make its mark on our writing in every direction, giving it depth and breadth—*i.e.*, we shall see below the surface instead of only recording the obvious; and take big views instead of indulging in puerilities and pettiness.

Likewise it should make us more tolerant and sympathetic and large-minded, knowing that life is not always what it seems.

And it may help us to accuracy—a virtue of priceless worth to the writer.

Of course, the knowledge acquired from the reading of great books does not take the place of the knowledge we gain by mixing with living people; we need the one as much as the other. But it is a wonderful help in enlarging our power of thinking, and the scope of our thoughts; and it opens our eyes to much in the world around us that we might otherwise miss.

So much by way of precept. Now for an example of the type of writing that is overloaded with learning.

Some years ago, when I was assistant-editor of the *Windsor Magazine*, a girl, who had taken her B.A., came to me with an urgent request that I would help her to a start in journalism. If only I would give her the smallest opening, she was sure she would get on; she was willing to try her hand at anything, if only—etc.

At the moment we were proposing to publish an article on the nearly extinct London "Cabby." I had already arranged with some typical cabmen to be at a certain cab-shelter on a given day, to be interviewed. As this girl was so keen to try her hand at writing up a given subject, I asked her if she would care to tackle the "Cabmen" article, explaining that we wanted a simple straightforward account of their work and experiences, the various drawbacks of the profession, any curiosities in the way of passengers they had come across, and similar particulars calculated to arouse public interest in the men.

She was charmed with the idea, and grateful for the chance to get a start. And she said she quite understood the simple, chatty style of article I wanted.

A week later the article arrived. And oh, how that girl had slaved over it, too; it seemed to me she had tried to include in it everything she knew! It started with an eight-line Greek quotation. It gave historical details of the city of London; there were references to Roman charioteers and the Olympic games, extracts from Chaucer and other authors equally respectable. Indeed, there seemed to be something of everything in the article—excepting information about the cabmen. What little she had written about them, poor men, was swamped by the display of her own knowledge.

Yet it was difficult to make her understand that there was something incongruous in the association of broken-down old cabmen with a Greek extract; that the one topic created a false atmosphere for the other; while equally it was unsuitable to introduce Greek into a general magazine, seeing that the larger proportion of the grown-ups among the reading public had forgotten all the Greek they ever knew.

Unpractised journalists are apt to overload their articles with data that has no immediate connection with the subject in hand, even though it may be distantly related. Such inclusions often weaken the whole, as they confuse rather than enlighten the reader.

One other caution is necessary. Avoid quoting from other people's writings. With some amateurs this amounts to a most irritating mania. Now and then, an apt quotation may serve to enforce a point, but the beginner should be sparing in their use.

Remember that people, as a rule, do not care to pay for what they have already read elsewhere! Also, a publisher only reckons to purchase original matter (apart from books that are avowedly compilations).

In any case, you are not gaining practice in original writing if you are merely copying out what some one else has written.

THE READER MUST BE INTERESTED

The first essential in any publication is that it shall interest people, especially the people who, it is hoped, will buy it. Every book does not appeal to the same type of reader; but every book should appeal to *some* type of reader, and it should interest that type of reader, or it will prove a failure.

This does not necessarily mean that it must keep the reader wrought up to a high pitch of excitement, or squirming with laughter, or bathed in tears—though a judicious mixture of these things may contribute much to the success of your work. It means that what you propose to tell people must be something they will want to hear; and when you start to tell it to them, you must tell it in such a way that they will be keen for you to continue.

Beginners often think the main point is their own interest in what they write. It is certainly desirable that we ourselves should be interested in what we write, otherwise the chances are it will not be worth reading; but it is still more important that what we write should interest other people. I have known a book to sell well, though the author was thoroughly bored when writing it; but I have never known a book to sell well if the public were thoroughly bored when trying to read it!

IF YOUR WRITINGS DO NOT GRIP, THEY WILL NOT SELL

And this necessity for interesting the reader applies to every class of writing. It is useless to write a scientific treatise in such a dull way that the student is not sufficiently attracted to read the second chapter; it is useless to write a religious article in such a stereotyped, conventional manner that nobody gets beyond the second paragraph, and everybody is quite willing to take the rest as read; it is useless to write such vague insipid verse that the reader does not even take the trouble to find out what it is all about; and it is useless to write feeble fiction that lands the reader nowhere in particular, at the end of several chapters.

If you cannot grip, and then hold, the reader's attention, your writings will not be read.

And if they are not read, they will not sell.

You may think this last remark a backward way of putting it, and that a book must sell before it can be read. But several people read it before a copy is actually sold, and often a good deal depends on the verdict of these people. It is read by the publisher, or his editor (sometimes several of them); if they decide that it does not interest them, and that it is not likely to interest the public—where are you?

Even if you determine, after your Ms. has been declined by a few dozen publishers, to pay for its publication yourself, and in this way get it into print, there are the reviewers to be thought of; should they be of the same opinion as the publishers who declined it, and find it so lacking in interest that they never trouble to finish it, and ignore it entirely in their review columns—that, again, is unfortunate for you!

Among other people who may read it, there are the publisher's travellers. If it fails to interest them they can hardly grow so enthusiastic over it, when displaying it to the bookseller, as they do over another book that kept them sitting up all night to finish it!

More than this, a keen, intelligent bookseller reads many of the books on his counter, in order that he may know what to recommend his customers when they ask him for a book of a definite type. Indeed, he is often supplied with "advance copies" by the publisher. If he finds a volume engrossing, you may rely on his introducing it to his customers; and if the purchasers of the earliest copies are captivated by it, they will certainly talk about it and urge their acquaintances to read it, and send it to their friends on dates when gifts are due.

Thus you see a book really must be read before it has a chance of any sale.

Beginners often think the all-important thing is to get their Ms. set up in type; that once it is published the public will buy it and read it as a matter of course. But the public won't, unless it interests them. And no matter how much money an author may be able to expend on the production of a book, it will bring him little satisfaction if that book does not sell, and he sees the major portion of the edition eventually cleared out as a "remainder," or dumped in stacks on his door-step, when the publisher can give it shelf-room no longer.

THE PERSONAL OUTLOOK MUST BE TAKEN INTO ACCOUNT

To interest people you must write on subjects of which they know something, or subjects which in some way make an appeal to them. You seldom succeed in interesting them if you write of things quite outside their usual range of thought or ideals or aspirations. To ensure some attention from your audience, it is impera-tive that this matter of personal outlook be taken into account.

A subject may be of enthralling interest to you, but if it is not in any way likely to interest your readers from a personal standpoint—if it has no connection with their spiritual or material life, if it makes no appeal to them on the score of beauty, if they cannot by any stretch of imagination see themselves in a leading part—then it is risky to make that the subject of an early article or book. When you are well-established, and recognised as a capable writer, you can take your chance with any exotic subject you please; but I do not advise it at the beginning of your career.

This does not mean that out-of-the-way subjects should never be chosen. Obviously life would be deadly monotonous if we were always trotting round the same circle. Novelty is most desirable; monotony is fatal to success. But it must be novelty that is linked in some way with the reader's life.

Let us suppose you are absorbed in the study of a certain new germ—a germ that is responsible for much mortality among tadpoles. Not only have you discovered the existence of this germ but you have taken its name and address, inspected its birth certificate, secured its photograph, insisted on knowing its age and where the family go to school, ascertained its average food ration, noted its climatic preferences, and many other useful facts. All this would be very interesting to persons who are rearing frogs; but as such people are few in number, it would scarcely attract the bulk of the reading public, hence you could not expect a book on the subject to have a large sale; nor would an article be likely to find a resting place in a magazine or newspaper that aimed to attract the general public. The subject would have no interest for the majority of people, because once we have left our unscientific youth behind, tadpoles are generally as remote from our life as the North Pole.

But, suppose you suddenly discover that these same germs are communicated by tadpoles to water-cress, and therefore directly responsible for hay fever or whooping-cough (or something equally conclusive); you will find the general public all attention in an instant, since water-cress and whooping-cough make a personal claim on most of us. And in that case your writings would find a market at once.

A Novel must have "Grit" Somewhere in its Composition

The same ruling applies to fiction. Study any successful novelist, and you will see how his knowledge of the things that appeal to men and women guided him in the choice of a subject, and his manner of presenting it.

Some beginners think a peculiar plot, or a bizarre background, or an eccentric subject is more likely to command attention than familiar topics; but that depends entirely on what there is in it likely to appeal to the reader and rivet his attention. Mere eccentricity or peculiarity will not in itself ensure the reader's permanent interest; behind the externals there must be something with more "grit" in it.

While newness of idea is much to be desired, and a breaking-away from hackneyed scenes and types should be aimed for, there must be a strong underlying link to connect the unusual idea with the reader's sympathies and mental attitude. You may lay the scene of your story in the Stone Age, or make your hero and heroine some never-heard-of-before dwellers in the moon; but unless you can interweave some fundamental human trait, or some soul longing that will make such a story understandable to ordinary humanity, it will not interest average readers, since they know very little about the tastes and manners and customs of the folks who lived in the Stone Age; neither are they likely to be at all convinced, nor particularly excited, because you tell them certain circumstances about beings, said to be in the moon, who could never possibly come their way.

Mere Eccentricity will not hold the Public

Even though a few people may at first be attracted by some eccentricity on your part (and, after all, if we only shriek loud enough, some one is certain to turn round and look at us), there is no lasting quality in such methods of catching attention.

A troupe of pierrots at the seaside may get themselves up in a garb bizarre enough to give points to the cubists; but unless they also provide a fair programme, they will not retain an audience. After the first glance at their peculiarities, the public will stroll farther along the parade to the much plainer-looking company, if that company provide a better entertainment.

There must be "body" in the goods you offer the public, apart from qualities that are only superficial, such as a weird or unusual setting.

In some cases an author's strong appeal to human interest has even borne him aloft over actual defects.

Why Fame has sometimes Overlooked Defects

The verses of Ann and Jane Taylor could never be called poetry; yet most of the incidents recorded touch a sympathetic chord in every child's life, and each "moral" emphasises exactly the claims of justice that are recognised with surprising clearness by even the youngest; hence the poems have a personal interest for any normal, healthy-minded child. And, in consequence, they have lived for over a hundred years.

In certain of his books Ruskin wrote much about pictures—pictures that could only interest a small proportion of the general public, because so few are able to go and see the pictures in the Continental churches and galleries. Moreover, some of his art criticism is considered worthless by many artists. Yet Ruskin has been, and still is, universally read. Why?

Because, in addition to his erroneous estimate of certain artists, and his prejudices against others, and his remarks about unfamiliar pictures many of his readers have never seen, he continually touched on matters in which we all have a very personal interest—our duty to God, our relations to our fellow-men, the inner workings of our mind, the problems of the soul, the beauties and messages of Nature, and scores of other topics that are of the keenest interest to every thoughtful person. Ruskin himself complained that people did not read him for what he had to say, but for the way in which he said it. Yet he was not quite correct in this. People read him for something besides his style; they often read him for the side issues, the comments by the way, the little vignettes and pen-pictures of scenery, the great truths embodied in a few sentences—matters that strike home to us all, even when the main purport of a book may appeal only to a few.

Having recognised the need for interesting the reader, decide next the means by which you hope to do this.

DECIDE THE MEANS BY WHICH YOU WILL ENDEAVOUR TO INTEREST

It may be a merry jingle nonsense rhymes that you intend shall please by their very absurdity; or it may be the voicing of some tragedy haunting many human lives that you rely on to touch the human heart; or the description of some scene of beauty that you feel will be the main attraction of your writing; or perhaps it is the unselfishness of the hero, the strong courage of the heroine, or the ingenuity of the villain that is to be its outstanding feature.

Whatever it may be—keep it well in view, and always work up to it. The trouble with so many amateurs is their tendency to forget, before they are half-way through their Ms., the ideas with which they started!

SETTLE ON YOUR AUDIENCE

The class of reader whom you hope to attract is another point to be taken into consideration. The literature that appeals to the factory girl is not the type calculated to enthuse the business man; the book that delights the Nature lover might be voted "insufferably dull" by the woman who likes to fancy herself indispensable to smart society.

While we do not, as a rule, write only for one small section of society, there are certain divisions, nevertheless, that must be recognised; and the beginner who is not sufficiently versed in his craft to be able to work in broad sweeps on a big canvas that can be seen and understood by all, is wise to observe definite limitations, and work within a clearly-marked area.

You must decide whether a story is for the schoolgirl or her mother; whether you are writing for those who crave sensation, or for those who like quiet, thoughtful, restrained reading; whether your article is for the student who already knows something about the matter, or for the general reader whom you wish to interest in your theme.

Having settled who are to be your readers—do not let them slip your memory while you address several other conflicting audiences from time to time. Writers of books for children are especial sinners in this respect, frequently introducing passages that are quite outside the child's purview, and obviously better suited to adults.

BE SURE OF YOUR OBJECT

Your object in writing should be definitely settled before you start on your Ms. Is it to instruct, or to help, or to entertain? Is it to provide excitement, or to act as a soothing restorative to tired nerves and brain? Is it to expose some social wrong, or to enlist sympathy for suffering and misfortune? Is it to make people smile, or to make them weep? Is it to induce a light-hearted and care-free frame of mind, or to make the reader think? Is it to pander to a vicious taste, or to foster clean ideals?

Inexperienced writers often seem to think there is no need for any defined purpose in their work, unless they are issuing an appeal for charity, or writing an article that is to combat some special evil. Yet everything we write should have a purpose. Unfortunately, we have dropped into a habit of ticketing a work "a book with a purpose" when it deals particularly with religious or social propaganda; whereas every book should be a book with a purpose, or it will not be worth the paper it is written upon. You must have some reason for what you write, or some object which you keep in view, if you are to make any impression on the reader.

Many of you who are beginners will probably explain that your object in writing is solely to entertain (and a very good object it is). In that case, see to it that your writing *is* entertaining. Don't let it be flat and colourless and tepid for pages at a stretch.

But you must remember that every book should be entertaining. This is as much a primary necessity as that every book should be grammatical. It is another way of saying that every book must interest people. Yet how few amateurs stop to consider whether what they write is really entertaining?

Ask yourself, after your Ms. is completed, "If I saw this in print, should I be so impressed with it that I should write off at once to my friends and urge them to buy it, and mention it to all my acquaintances as something well worth their getting and reading?" If not—why not?

If you can criticise your own work dispassionately in this way, it will help you to detect some of your own weak points. But, unfortunately, so few of us can look dispassionately upon the children of our own brain!

FORM SHOULD BE CONSIDERED

Form which plays a very important part in the construction of literature, means shape and order; it means also definite restrictions.

Though we do not realise it at first, these restrictions are particularly desirable. Without them, we might go writing on and on, till no one could follow us in our meanderings, the brain would be worn-out with the attempt. Yet these same restrictions are what the novice most resents, or at any rate is inclined to flout.

Nevertheless, you must abide by certain rules if your work is to be readable and profitable.

ESTABLISHED RULES SAVE OUR WASTING TIME ON EXPERIMENTS

You may regard all rules as arbitrary. I know how inclined one is, when only just beginning to feel one's feet, to kick down every sort or prop and barrier and sign-post and ledge, in order to run riot, without let or hindrance, over all the earth. But we cannot do this when we are only learning to walk, without tumbling down and acquiring bruises; and then we lose a certain amount of time in picking ourselves up and getting our bearings again.

While the thought of starting out on brand-new adventure, without any one's advice or dictation, is very enticing, the wise person is he who first of all avails himself of the discoveries already made by other folk (a time-saving policy to say the least of it). Then, when he has assimilated as much as he can of what others before him have found out, he can experiment on his own, and start on a voyage of discovery into truly unknown lands. But it is sheer waste of energy to go pioneering over land that has already been thoroughly investigated, and mapped out, by men and women who have gone before us.

And although we may consider the limitations of Form in Art as quite superfluous in our own particular case, it is well to get thoroughly acquainted with them, bearing in mind the fact that thousands of writers for centuries past have been handling the subject, experimenting along these same lines, often asking the same questions that we are asking. And all whose opinions were worth anything came to the same conclusion, viz:—that strict attention to Form is necessary in all creative work, if that work is to have lasting value.

Therefore you might as well accept this at the outset, at any rate until you have reached the stage where you can do exactly as you please and still command the attention of an admiring universe.

THE THREE-PART BASIS

All the master-minds seem to agree that a story, whether long or short, should consist of three main parts. Indeed most of the art-products of the brain are constructed on a three-part basis. Experience has shown that this form is the most satisfying to the mind—and remember, one of the essentials of a work of art is that it shall satisfy the mind with that sense of fitness and completeness and appropriateness, so very hard to define exactly in words, and yet so necessary to our enjoyment of anything.

A painting has foreground, middle distance and background. A musical composition, if short, has generally a first part in one key, a second part in the minor or a related key, and a third part that is often an amplification of the first part with additional matter that brings it to a satisfactory conclusion. If the composition be lengthy, such as a sonata or symphony, its First Movement, Slow Movement and Finale are labeled for all to understand.

The three-volume novel of our grandmothers' day was a recognition of the desirability of definite division. And although we do not now spread our stories over so much paper, nor trim them with such wide margins and three sets of covers, the three parts are still there, and in many cases the author still marks them plainly for the reader, by dividing his work into specified sections.

Sometimes we find a 4th Act, and a 5th, in a play, just as we sometimes have four movements in a sonata; but in most cases the extra act is really only an episode, not a main division in itself, and usually belongs to the second part.

The Divisions of a Story

Broadly speaking, the divisions of a story may be ticketed—

1. Starting things.
2. Developing things.
3. Accomplishing things.

The first part is devoted to introducing the characters; starting them to work, according to some pre-arranged scheme in the author's mind; laying in the background, and generally "getting acquainted."

In the second part, the scheme or plot is developed; complications and side issues, contrasting episodes and by-play may be introduced. This is the place for the author to exercise all his ingenuity in seeming to wander farther and farther from the solution of the problem of the story, while in reality he is ever drawing the reader towards it.

The third part is concerned with the actual solution of the problem, and shows how all the previous happenings helped to bring about the climax with which the story should end.

Length Must Be Taken into Consideration

The three parts may, or may not, be about equal in length; but if one is longer than the other, it should be the middle part. It is never well to introduce delays in the first part, nor are they desirable in the last part.

To be complex or episodical at the start is unwise; the reader likes to get well under way moderately early, to know who everybody is and what they are after. When your story is fairly launched, you can lengthen it with diversions, descriptions, dialogues, and episodes, and, granted they are interesting and have a direct bearing on the story, the reader will not complain.

But once you reach the third part, and start to gather up the scattered characters and far-flung incidents, in order to unite them all into one convincing conclusion, you must not dally, nor divert the reader's attention from the main issue.

You will see from the foregoing that it is necessary to fix the length of your story before you start to work—otherwise you will not get it properly balanced. I do not mean that you must tie yourself down to an exact number of words for each part, any more than for the whole; but you should settle, before you start, an approximate estimate of the amount of space you will allow to each part, and then see that you keep somewhere near it.

For instance, the probability is that, unless you keep an eye on yourself, you will overdo the detail in the first part. So many novices start writing their story before they have half thought it out in all its bearings; the result is that all sorts of new ideas come to them, and fresh developments, and different aspects of the plot; and they add to their original plan, work in fresh characters, amplify those that are already there, till all sense of proportion is gone. Or they may have a special liking for one particular character (invariably it is the one who, they secretly think, represents their own tastes and aspirations), and they will overdo this one with detail, and unduly spin out that portion of the book.

Then again, when we are fresh, and only starting a work, we are more inclined to stroll leisurely among voluminous particulars, and write all that comes into our head, than we are when we have written forty thousand words, and are wishing we could get the rest of it out of our brain, and down on the paper, with less physical, as well as less mental, effort!

Therefore, when you eventually revise your Ms. as a whole, overhaul the first section very thoroughly, cutting it down ruthlessly if you find you have been unduly diffuse.

Nowadays a story that drags at the outset is doomed.

Form as Applied to Articles

But fiction is not the only class of writing ruled by Form; articles, essays, verse are all subject to a certain order of presentation, and certain restrictions, which no writer can ignore without lessening the effectiveness of his work—and in the main the threefold basis applies to all.

When writing an essay or an article, it is useful to make your divisions as follows—

1. State your theme and your reasons for its choice. (In other words: make it quite clear to your readers what you are going to write about, and why you decided to write about it.)
2. Say what you have to say about it.
3. Give the conclusions to be drawn therefrom.

Here, as in the case of fiction, it is desirable to get right into your subject quickly, never "side-tracking" the readers' mind on to a subsidiary topic until they have a firm hold of your main theme. Ruskin was particularly tiresome in the way he would turn off at a tangent, and start talking about some minor matter, before the reader had grasped what subject he was proposing to deal with.

After you have turned your theme inside out, in the second part, and told all the points about it that you think will be new to your reader, make your third part a climax, in that it works up to a definite conclusion.

It does not matter what the subject of your article, broadly speaking it should be built on these lines, since this is the form in which the human mind seems best able to take in information. You cannot expect people to follow your descriptions, your arguments, or your objections, if they do not know what you are talking about; hence the need for a very clear presentation of your subject at the beginning.

And, in order to leave your reader in a satisfied frame of mind, *i.e.* with a sense of certainty that things were brought to their logical conclusion—also an essential in a work of art—the third section must be primarily occupied with the reasons for, or the outcome of, or the deductions to be drawn from, that which has gone before.

This leaves the middle section of the article for digressions, side issues, or any other form of amplification.

Once the student recognises how desirable are the laws of Form, how they give shape and proportion and cohesion to matter that would otherwise be void and hopeless, he will realise how impossible it is to do good work without preliminary thought, and careful planning. And he will also understand how it is that Mss. which are merely "dashed off" without any preparatory work, those that "just came of their own accord," as the authors sometimes boast, invariably fail to arouse a spark of enthusiasm in the soul of an editor.

Right Selection Is Important

The mere fact that the sun never sets on the British Empire does not necessitate our including the whole of it in one Ms. Yet some beginners seem most industriously anxious to do this.

Amateurs may be divided roughly into two classes: those who tell too little, and those who tell too much. The majority come under the latter heading. The literary artist is he who knows exactly what to select from the mass of material before him (in order to make the reader see what he himself sees); and what to discard as non-essential.

I am inclined to think that the instinct for selection is largely born, not made. It is one of the channels through which genius betrays itself. Very few great artists can explain why they chose one particular set of items for their canvas, or their book, and ignored others; or why that particular set conveys a sense of beauty to the observer, when another set would make no such appeal.

Yet the sense or instinct can be cultivated to some extent, and the first step is to recognise the necessity for careful selection. Few beginners give a thought to the matter. They imagine that all they have to do, when they set out to tell a story, or describe some incident or scene, is to say all they can about it—the more the better.

"I never spare myself where detail is concerned," a would-be contributor wrote when offering a magazine article. Unfortunately she did not spare me either; there were fifty-seven pages of close, nearly illegible writing, describing the tombs of some long-dead unknowns in an out-of-the-way Continental church.

To enumerate every single item is not Art; it is cataloguing.

Slight themes require but few details.

TRAINING YOURSELF IN THE MATTER OF SELECTION

Look your subject well over before you write a line; decide what are its outstanding features, which are its most prominent characteristics, and what it is absolutely necessary to say about it, in order to give a clear presentment. At the same time, note what is irrelevant to the main purport of your writing, and what is comparatively unimportant.

After all, the mind can only take in a certain amount of detail, a certain number of facts; and as it cannot absorb everything, a limit has to be placed somewhere. Common sense tells us that since something must be left out, it is well to omit the colourless, unimportant data that never will be missed!

In every scene there are always definite points that arrest the attention and give character to the whole, and many other points that really do not make very much difference one way or the other. The artist (whether he be making word-pictures or colour-pictures) selects those points that give the most character to the scene, those incidents which convey the most comprehensive idea of the place and the people and their doings, in the fewest words.

If you are writing a story, it is seldom necessary to describe every thing appertaining to, and every one connected with, the heroine, for example—at any rate, not on her first appearance. Her home, her relations, her dress, can often be dealt with in a few sentences; but those sentences must contain just the facts that give the key to the whole situation.

Probably it will not throw any vivid light on the lady if you state that her drawing-room was upholstered in old rose, and she herself devoted to chocolate; because the virtuous no less than the wicked, the most advanced feminist as well as the silliest bundle of vanity, might all have equal leanings toward old rose and be addicted to chocolate. But if you state, either that she was reading a first edition of Dante, or cutting out flannelette undergarments for the sewing meeting, or powdering her chalky nose in public—the reader will have some sort of clue as to your heroine's personality. An instinct for selection will tell you which item will characterise a person most accurately.

In the same way some incidents will directly affect the whole trend of a story, others leave the main issues untouched. Select the incidents that matter, and leave those that merely mark time without taking the reader any further.

Caricature is not Characterization

But while it is desirable to record outstanding features, it is not wise, as a rule, to emphasise mere peculiarities, as this only tends to stamp one's writing as unnatural, exaggerated, or caricature. Far better seize on general topical characteristics, only select those that are prominent, colourful, and vigorous, rather than neutral, insipid traits or happenings.

People reading Kipling's story, "The Cat that walked by itself," invariably exclaim, "That's just like *our* cat!" Yet in all probability Kipling's cat was not at all like either of their cats. He merely chose the typical characteristics common to all cats, and each person immediately sees his own individual pussy in the picture.

A lack of an instinct for selection is one of the commonest failings in amateurs, and is responsible for the rejection of an endless stream of Mss. For this reason it is desirable that the beginner should pay special heed to the subject, and note to what extent he is making actual selection, or whether he is merely jotting down all and sundry in haphazard unconcern.

When Writing Articles

There are two main difficulties in writing an article; one is to get a good beginning, the other is to get a good ending. If you know your subject well (and it is useless to write on a subject you do not know well), it is wonderful how the middle portion takes care of itself in comparison with the care that has to be bestowed on the entrance and exit.

I have seen amateurs write and write and re-write their opening paragraphs (with intervals of perplexed pen-nibbling in between), crossing out a sentence as soon as they put it down, interpolating fresh ideas that ran off at a tangent, suddenly jumping back a hundred years or so in their anxiety to start at the very beginning of the subject—and finally tearing up their by-now-unreadable Ms., and commencing all over again.

Here are two methods by which you may more easily get under way—and the great thing is to get under way, and write *something*, then you at least have a concrete Ms. to pull to pieces and re-arrange and hammer into shape. It is the blank paper, or the page you have crossed out and then torn up in despair, that is so irritatingly non-productive!

Settle your Chronological Starting-point—and Stick to it

Decide, before you write a line, the exact point in the life-story of your subject at which you will start. Remember that it is impossible to say *everything* about it, or give the whole of its history; therefore settle quickly what can safely be left out concerning its antecedents and early childhood without detriment to the subject as a whole.

Once you have made up your mind as to the precise chronological starting point, stick to it (half the initial trouble of getting into your subject will be over if you do); and do not in the course of a few paragraphs hark back to some previous happening or era, because you have suddenly remembered something that might be made to bear on the subject.

The way anxious writers will endeavour to tell every mortal thing that can be told regarding the most distant prehistoric family connections of their subject, is on a par with a certain type of chairman at a meeting, who will persist in dilating on the sayings and doings of his great-grandfather instead of dealing with the topic in hand.

If I ask the untrained amateur to write me an article on "The Use of Pigeons in War," the chances are all in favour of his starting with the Ark, and talking for several paragraphs round the Dove with the olive branch. By a natural and easy transition, he would presently be quoting, "Oh for the wings of a dove!" Pliny's doves would have an innings, the London pigeons of St. Paul's have honourable mention, the ornithological significance of the botanical term *Aquilegia* might be touched upon, with other equally irrelevant or far-fetched allusions to the *Columbæ* as a whole; and all this before any really serviceable information is forthcoming under the heading specified.

This is no exaggerated picture; it is the type of article frequently submitted, and is due to a writer's lack of an instinct for selection, and his determination to leave nothing unsaid. In the end, he of course leaves a great deal unsaid, because the inevitable limitations of an article make it impossible to give so much past history and still find room to say what should be said about the present-day aspect. The space is gone before the writer has barely got there!

And because of this tendency to expend too much ink at the beginning on details that are too far removed from the central point of interest to be worth recording, I will give another hint that may occasionally prove useful.

WHEN IN DOUBT—BEGIN IN THE MIDDLE

When in doubt where to start, begin in the middle; *i.e.* attack the subject where the interest seems to focus; or launch out without any preliminary whatever, into the very heart of the matter. It is quite possible it may prove to be the beginning!

The desirability of shaping an article according to the definite rules of form was dealt with on page 136. A careful planning of the form beforehand will help the writer to keep his article properly balanced, and to avoid over-weighting it unduly with unimportant data at the outset.

WHEN YOU HAVE FINISHED—LEAVE OFF

With regard to the wind-up of an article, here again the writer has much in common with the speaker, and happy is he who knows instinctively just when to leave off. So few do!

Failing an instinctive perception of the right ending, or the desirable climax, the writer can deliberately plan one and then work up to it. And it is well to plan it fairly early, in order to make the whole of the article gravitate toward this finale.

It is the Final Impression that Counts

In writing, as in so many other things, it is the final impression that counts. The reader's attitude of mind, when he comes to the end of the last page, is a powerful factor in settling your success as a writer. If you end lamely, with non-effective sentences, or with pointless indecision—if, in short, the reader does not feel he has got somewhere or achieved something by reading the article, he will not be remarkably keen on anything else you may write.

The beginner seldom pauses to inquire: What is my object in writing this article? If I were to put the question to a number of would-be authors, and they replied truthfully, they would say, "To see myself in print," or, "To make money"; yet I cannot reiterate too often that what we write must have more in the way of backbone than this. The reason that thousands of Mss. are returned to the senders every year is because those senders had no other object in view, apart from money-making or getting into print.

Decide therefore on a more useful object—useful, that is, from the reader's point of view. The reader does not care one iota whether you are going to make money, or whether you now see yourself in print for the first time. The point *he* is concerned with is what he himself gets out of his reading—whether he has been amused and entertained, or has gained information, or a new light on an old subject, or a spiritual uplift, or useful facts, or some fresh interest, or a soothing narcotic for an anxious brain.

And you must have some such object in mind, when you plan the shortest article, no less than when you scheme out a novel.

In writing the article on "The Use of Pigeons in War" your object might be the giving of information that would be fresh to the public (and we never need trouble to tell them that which they know already); information calculated to increase their knowledge of the ways in which we waged the great war for the world's freedom, and also to give them a new interest in these wonderful birds. Bearing all this in mind, it will be seen at once that the preamble about the Ark would be quite unnecessary, since it would convey no new information whatever.

Mere recapitulation of ancient well-known facts is never desirable, outside a text-book.

Keep an Eye on Topicality

Topicality has often much to do with the acceptance of an article; but the beginner seldom takes this point into consideration. The finest article one could write would be turned down if the subject were out of date—and twenty-four hours make all the difference. We move at such express speed, and events hurry past at such a rapid rate, that the article an editor would jump at to-day may be useless to him to-morrow; the book that would be marketable this season may be unsaleable next.

Of course this does not apply to every Ms., but it does to a good many, and particularly in regard to articles for periodicals. If you think your subject will have special interest for the public at the moment—send it at once, and if it is the burning question of the day, send it to a newspaper rather than to a magazine, remembering that magazines have to go to press some weeks before the date of publication. If a magazine editor receives your Ms. January 1st, the very earliest he could get it into his magazine would probably be April, and the chances are he would have everything planned and set up until May. In the *Girls' Own Paper and Woman's Magazine*, for instance, the final sheet of the September number has to be passed for press the first week in June.

Bearing these facts in mind, you will realise that it is useless to send an article on a Christmassy subject to an editor in November. His Christmas number was probably put together in August, and by November it is travelling by train or steamer, bullock-wagon or native carrier, to distant parts of the world.

ARTICLES THAT ARE NOT WANTED

And I must mention another fault common with beginners. It is useless to offer articles that are nothing more than a *réchauffé* of encyclopædic facts. Any schoolboy can string together text-book information, and compile facts from other people's works.

If your article is on an old-established theory, or some well-known theme, you must contribute some new personal experience, if it is to be of any worth. Readers will not pay for books or articles that contain nothing but what they could write themselves, given the time and the works of reference.

Then, again, it is useless to choose a subject merely because it appeals to you personally; if there is no likelihood of its appealing to the majority of the readers, it is valueless to an editor.

STUDY THE READERS' PREFERENCE NO LESS THAN YOUR OWN

The business of writing is like every other business in that self-effacement may contribute much to success. The good business man does not spend his time talking about his own tastes and achievements and preferences; he keeps an eye on what interests his customers and talks about that.

The good writer does not write merely to air his own likes and dislikes and grievances, or to impress people with his own attainments and good fortune; he keeps his eye on what interests his readers (who are his customers) and follows this up in some degree in his writings.

This need not mean any relinquishing of personal ideals, or pandering to cheap tastes. The readers' ideals may be as high—or even higher—than yours; their tastes may be quite as refined—but they are not necessarily the same as yours. Therefore, study what will interest them to read rather than what it will interest you that they should read. Think it out, and you will find there may be a world of difference between the two.

Send Suitable Articles to Likely Magazines

Writers are often told to study the type of articles appearing in the magazine in which they are anxious to see their own work published. This is very sound advice. The unsuitabilities that are offered at times are past counting. A man wrote recently to the editor of a prominent Missionary Monthly: "I notice you have no chess columns in your paper. I could supply one regularly, and I assure you it would help your circulation considerably." For the *Woman's Magazine* I have been offered murder stories of the most lurid and revolting character; articles on "Seal-hunting in the Arctic as a Sport," "Curiosities in Kite-Flying," "The Making of Modern Motor Roads," and others equally outside the range of women's activities even in these days of wide-flung doors.

Editors do not want Repeat-Subjects as a Rule

Avoid offering articles on subjects that have already been dealt with in a periodical. Unless you have unique and valuable information to add to that already given, space cannot be spared to repeat matter. Moreover, the public does not want to pay twice for the same thing—and that is what it would amount to.

It is no recommendation to write to an editor, "I see you have an article on 'Glow-worms as a Hat-Trimming' in your last issue; I am therefore sending you another article on the same subject." Unless you have some new and really informing data to contribute, the probability is that you would only be covering the same ground as the previous writer.

Neither are you likely to get your Ms. accepted if you write, "I have read the article on 'Glow-worms' in your last issue, and disagree with many of the statements made therein. Far from glow-worms being things of elusive beauty and suggestive of fairyland, as your contributor calls them. I regard them as noxious pests. I have written my views in detail, and hope you will be able to publish the article in your next issue to counteract the wrong impression that the other one conveyed."

Now, an editor to a large extent identifies himself with the views expressed in the pages of the paper he edits. And had he not approved of the statements made, he would not have been inclined to print them in an ordinary non-controversial paper. Is it likely, then, that he would want another contribution calmly informing his readers that the previous article was entirely wrong and unreliable?

On The Subject of "How to——"

Most editors are overdone with the usual "How to—" articles. The public has by now been told "How to" do everything under the sun, I am inclined to think;

but if you feel it laid upon your soul to impart still further instruction—try to find a fresh form of title.

Do not choose too big a subject. "Heaven," "Human Nature," "Eternity," and kindred themes are beyond the powers of any mortal—much less the beginner.

Get right away from hackneyed phrases and allusions. So many Mss. are peppered throughout with such expressions as "all sorts and conditions"; "common or garden"; "let us return to our muttons"; "tell it not in Gath"; "but we must not anticipate."

If you feel drawn to write an essay on "Friendship," it is not necessary to start with David and Jonathan; they have already been mentioned—more than once, in fact—in this connection. Neither is it desirable, when writing about Jerusalem to quote, "a city that is set on a hill cannot be hid."

Variety is always pleasing, and editors do like to come upon something, occasionally, that they have not read more than a dozen times before.

SUGGESTIONS FOR STYLE

If you are writing with the object of giving information, avoid the indefinite style. Either make a clear, decided statement (if you are competent to do so), or leave the matter alone. You not only weaken the force of your statements, and smudge your meaning, by beating about the bush and walking round your subject, but you cast doubts in the reader's mind as to whether you are fully qualified to write about it at all.

Here is an extract from an article sent to me on "The Cultivation of Broad Beans." Speaking of blight, the writer says: "I would not presume to dictate to the experienced gardener, who doubtless has his own method of dealing with the black blight that is so common on these plants; but for the benefit of the novice I would say that, personally, I always find it a good plan to nip off the tops of the beans so soon as the black fly appears. And, failing a better plan, the amateur might try this."

Articles written in this strain are fairly common, and are often the outcome of modesty on the part of a writer who does not wish to appear too dogmatic, or "to take too much upon himself." But from the utility point of view they are poor stuff, and are suffering as much from "blight" as the unfortunate beans, since each statement seems to be disparaged in some way by the over-diffident author!

Either the remedy suggested for the black fly *is* a remedy, or it isn't. If it is a remedy, then it is as applicable to the bean owned by the experienced gardener as to the one owned by the novice. In short—if it be advantageous to nip off the tops of blighted broad beans, the writer should have said so in simple English, without apologising for his temerity in making the statement, and thereby discounting all he says.

Ambiguity Must Not Be Allowed to Pass

Aim at writing with accuracy, clearness and precision. Ambiguity should never be allowed to pass. Any sentence that you feel to be in the slightest degree uncertain, or obscure, as to meaning should be reworded so as to leave no doubt whatever as to your meaning.

If, on re-reading your article, you are not quite sure what you meant when you wrote any passage, take it out altogether. Do not leave it in to puzzle the reader, even though you add a footnote—as Ruskin did—explaining that you have no idea what you meant when you wrote it.

In order to avoid an ambiguous style, two things are necessary: the ability to think clearly and concisely, and the ability to write down exactly what one thinks.

The Subject Should Regulate the Choice of Words

The choice of words should be influenced by the subject of your writing. A dignified subject calls for dignified language. A racy subject calls for racy language; and so on.

If your theme be a lofty one, do not "let down" the train of lofty thought it should engender, by introducing some word or phrase that induces a much lower—or a different—plane of thought and ideas. It is a backward policy, to say the least of it, to weaken, or obliterate, by ill-chosen language, the ideas you set out to foster in the reader. It is no extenuation to plead that the jarring phrase is particularly expressive; if it actually counteracts the ideas you seek to convey, it cannot be expressing your meaning.

The beginner often gets himself tied up in a knot with negatives; and even if he steer clear of actual error, he is apt to overdo himself with double negatives. It is better to make a direct statement in the affirmative if possible, than to involve it in negatives.

Instead of saying "a not uncommon fault," it is clearer at first sight if you say "a common fault," or "a fairly common fault." I know it does not always follow that the exact reverse fulfils the purpose of the double negative; a fault may be "not uncommon" and yet not exactly common. Nevertheless it is always possible to get the precise shade of meaning in the affirmative; and until a writer is quite fluent, it is better not to risk confusing the reader's mind by the introduction of too many negatives.

The Tendency to Use Involved Sentences

In the praiseworthy desire to use fine English, the beginner is very apt to get a sentence such a mixed-up maze of words that there seems little hope of the meaning ever getting out alive at the other end!

I take this from a Ms. just to hand:—

"Not that her parents would have entirely agreed with the supposition that there might have been that in his character which, had he not felt himself unequal to the task which affected him not a little in its apparent issue, even though actually simple in its ultimate object, it would have been possible for him to utilise to such an extent that he might not have entirely disappointed their none too sanguine estimate of his ability."

I admit that all amateurs do not rise to such cloud-wrapped heights; but many are nearly as bad!

Then, again, I have known the idea the author had in view when he started a paragraph, to get lost half-way through! This is due to the fact that the mind has not been trained to sustain consecutive thinking, but is permitted to veer round to all points of the compass like a weather-cock.

"EVERY WHY HATH A WHEREFORE"

If you enunciate a problem, see that you give the solution. If you start to elucidate some theory (or the reader is led to believe that you are going to elucidate it), do not forget all about it, and switch off to something else.

If you have no solution to offer, it is wiser and more satisfactory, as a general rule, not to put forward a problem at the close. A sense of incompleteness—or of something still awaiting fulfilment—is as disastrous to the success of an article as it is to the success of a book.

UNDESIRABLES

Beware of labouring a thought. If your point is only a slight one, do not reiterate it in various forms or over-embellish it.

If no big idea lies behind your sentences, no amount of impressive, ornate language will make your writing great.

People sometimes think that a fanciful style of writing will hide defects; whereas, on the contrary, it often emphasises them.

Avoid using many quotation marks and italics; they make a page look fidgety. Also they indicate weakness. If your remarks are not strong enough to stand alone, without words or phrases being propped up by quotes or underlinings, they are no better when so decorated.

A lavish use of extracts from other people's writings is undesirable. As I have said elsewhere, neither the publisher nor the reader is keen to pay for what they can read—and probably have already read—elsewhere.

A pedantic style of phraseology, and a desire to let other people see how much one knows, are amateur failings.

Some beginners go to the other extreme, and adopt a slangy, purposely-ungrammatical style, with the beginnings and finals of words clipped away, and a cultivated slovenliness that they imagine gives a picturesque quality, or an ultra up-to-dateness, to their writing.

But no good work is ever built on such foundations. The first thing to aim for is clarity, and the ability to express yourself in an easy, natural and concise manner, always using the fewest and the best words for the purpose, and employing them according to modern methods.

Improbabilities, misnamed "Imaginative Writing"

Amateurs often lean towards the improbable—calling it imaginative work—partly because they fancy they are less hampered by rules and restrictions than if they take everyday, mundane subjects. Yet—paradox though it may seem—the improbable must be bounded by probability in its own sphere; and imagination must be kept within definite limits and work according to definite forms—else it is no better than the gibberings of an unhinged mind.

Beginners frequently choose the moon, the stars, or the ether as the background for their imaginary characters; or they revel in after-death scenes that are supposed to represent the next world—either of suffering or of happiness. And a favourite ending is something like this, "Suddenly I awoke, and lo, it was only a dream," etc.

Avoid all these hackneyed themes, and obvious tricks.

It takes a Dante to lead us convincingly through the mazes of an unknown world.

Perhaps you feel that you are a Dante? Possibly you are: greatness must make a start somewhere. But in that case, there will be no need for you to strain after effect; genius can be evinced in the treatment of the simplest subjects.

Therefore experiment at the outset with everyday themes, and perfect your style in this direction before embarking on a very ambitious programme: we must learn to walk before we can run. The airman does not start turning somersaults the first time he goes aloft (or, if he does, that is the last time we hear of him, poor fellow).

It is a mistake to think that the undisciplined wanderings of an untrained mind betoken imaginative genius. It is the way one handles the commonplace that reveals the true artist; and style plays an important part in this, though it is by no means everything!

The question of imaginative work is big enough to deserve a volume to itself: much has already been written on the subject, and much remains to be said—too much to make it possible to do it justice in a book of this description. But I mention it here, in passing, to warn the beginner against spending much time on work that is not imaginative but merely impossible, until thoroughly grounded in the rudiments of his craft.

Pecularity is not Originality

Literature seldom gains by peculiarities of style or marked mannerisms, even though these are to be found in the works of certain writers who are of unquestionable ability. Such devices tend to become monotonous, and as a rule the public will only tolerate them when the subject matter of a book is so good that it is worth while to plough through the writer's mannerisms to get at it—*i.e.* mannerisms are put up with only when the writer is great in spite of them: no one is great because of his mannerisms; they are only superficial disturbances.

I am not saying this to discourage any attempt at originality of style; real originality is usually most desirable; what I am anxious to impress on the beginner is the fact that mere peculiarity is not originality.

Nor will it benefit anyone's work to copy the mannerisms of great writers—since these are often their defects.

MANNERISMS ARE SOON OUT OF DATE

It must also be remembered that many mannerisms are nothing more than fashions of the moment, just as most slang is; and in these rapid times they quickly become out of date, whereupon they give a book an antiquated touch. And few things are more difficult to survive than an atmosphere that is merely old-fashioned and nothing more.

It will be quite time enough, when you are expert at writing clear, understandable English, to decide whether your genius can best find expression in long and complicated sentences as used by Henry James, or in such cynical scintillations as those favoured by Bernard Shaw, OF in the paradoxical methods of G. K. Chesterton, or what you will. No limit need be set once a person has ideas to give the world, and can write them down in simple, direct, well-chosen language.

THE UBIQUITOUS FRAGMENT

Amateurs often think it is much easier to write a "fragment" than to write a complete anything. The one who hesitates as to whether he has the ability to write a long story, is quite sure he is capable of writing a fragmentary bit of fiction—one of those vague scraps with neither beginning nor ending that are always tumbling into the editor's letter-box—and he feels that all vagueness, and lack of finish, and the fact that the Ms. gets nowhere, are sanctioned because he adds, as a sub-title some such qualification as "An Episode," or "A Character Study," or "A Glimpse."

In the same way a writer who is too diffident to attempt a volume of essays, will feel perfect confidence in sending out a Ms. labelled "A Reverie," or "A Meditation," even though it be nothing more than a rambling collection of platitudes on the sunset.

In most cases it is a distrust of his own powers that inclines the amateur to embark on writing of this type.

A FRAGMENT MAY BE INCOMPLETE, BUT IT SHOULD NOT BE FORMLESS

Fragments may be exceedingly beautiful; they are really most acceptable in this hurrying age when life often seems too crowded with work-a-day cares to leave us much leisure for sustained reading. But they must embody the fundamental principles of Form; and they must be constructed with even more attention to artistic presentment, (or the means used to captivate the reader), than would be necessary for a lengthier work.

Also, though they are but fragmentary, they must appear to be portions of a desirable whole, sections of a well-finished piece of work. Their apparent incompleteness should seem due to the author having insufficient time—not insufficient knowledge—to finish them.

What is set down must not only be good work in itself, but it must suggest other good work as a completion.

You have probably seen some reproduction of a fragmentary pencil or pen-and-ink sketch, by an experienced artist, showing only a portion of a figure or a building; yet so suggestive that the onlooker instinctively fills in the remainder, and constructs out of the artist's unfinished drawing a picture complete and beautiful.

I have several such sketches before me on my study wall. One shows a corner of a quadrangle in the precincts of a cathedral. In the background there is a Gothic west window, a buttress, and a piece of a tower; while a flight of steps in a corner of the quadrangle, a bit of old-world stone-work around a doorway and window, a fragment of roof and a cluster of chimneys, with half a dozen lines indicating an ancient flagged walk, comprise the remainder. Only a few inches of paper and a few pen-strokes—nevertheless instinctively the mind runs on, and sees the whole of the cathedral in the shadowy background; the side of the quadrangle past the old doorway; even the street beyond with its cobble stones and market women. Indeed, you can visualise all the life of the quaint sleepy, French town if you look long enough at the little fragment; not because it is all indicated by the artist and left in an incomplete state, but because what he did put down is so vital, so suggestive, so fraught with possibilities, that the mind fills in all the blanks, and fills them in with beauty corresponding with the specimen he has shown us.

And while we are studying the sketch, it may be noticed that though this is but an unfinished fragment, it is perfectly balanced, and shapely and proportionate as it stands. The patch of light on the flagged path is balanced by the shadow in the doorway. The flight of crumbling stone steps, the most conspicuous feature in the foreground, has been drawn with the utmost pains in every detail. Even the cathedral window looming in the background has its exquisite tracery carefully drawn, no scamping the work because it was only the background of an incomplete sketch.

In the same way, a fragmentary word picture should be properly constructed, and absolutely accurate in detail (so far as that detail goes), well proportioned, carefully balanced, containing distinct charm in itself. The background may be only lightly indicated, but even so, it should contain possibilities—(the cathedral may be in misty shadow, but you must be able to see enough of it to know that it *is* a cathedral, and a great cathedral at that).

The central idea must be placed well in the foreground, it should be clearly stated, and be something worth calling an idea.

The points you mention, but leave unamplified should be something more than windowless, blank walls, or blind alleys leading nowhere; they should open up fresh vistas of thought, and send the reader's mind out and beyond the limits of your sentences.

Your word-picture must be satisfying in itself, even though one realises that it is but a small part of a much larger whole that might have been written, had time and space permitted.

Certain literary fragments extant are probably portions of large works the authors had in view but did not finish; Coleridge's "Kubla Khan," for instance. The type of fragment I am talking about in this chapter, however, is actually finished, so far as the author's handling is concerned; but unfinished in detail and setting, or with only a vignetted background.

Some writers have set down a few lines with neither introduction nor development plot, yet such is the force and the revealing quality of the sentences they put down, and the accuracy of their sense of selection, that they have conveyed as much, and suggested as much, to the mind of the reader as if they had written pages. The following verse of William Allingham is an example Here is a volume of suggestion in seven lines.

> Four ducks on a pond,
> A grass bank beyond,
> A blue sky of spring,
> White clouds on the wing:–
> What a little thing
> To remember for years–
> To remember with tears!

Tennyson wrote some beautiful fragments. "Flower in a Crannied Wall" contains a world of thought, and could easily furnish a theme for a row of ponderous books; "Break, break, break," has poignant possibilities.

William Sharp, as "Fiona Macleod," wrote some charming prose fragments; but behind each you will invariably find a complete idea, and an idea that suggests others.

Practise writing fragments by all means, but see that they are shapely, and suggestive of greater space and a bigger outlook than can be measured by the number of sentences. Above all, let each embody some idea—and let there be no uncertainty as to the whereabouts of that idea, no ambiguity as to what you are driving at.

To produce a good fragment you must do some intensive thinking, because you have not space to spread yourself out. This will be a gain to all your writing. The rambling, formless habit of thinking is the bane of the amateur, and the type of Mss. resulting therefrom is the bane of the editor.

Concerning Local Colour

Local colour can be a powerful factor in enhancing the charm of a story or article. It may be introduced as the background against which the scene is laid; or as a sidelight on the scenery, customs, and types of people peculiar to a district. Anything can be utilised that conjures up in the reader's mind the idiosyncrasies of a definite locality—only it must be something that *will* conjure up the scene.

One advantage of local colour is the opportunity it gives the writer of a double hold on the reader's interest—he may captivate by the setting of his theme no less than by the theme itself. Also it enables him more effectually to take the reader "out of himself," and place him in a new environment—an essential point if that reader is to become absorbed in what he is reading.

Mere verbatim description of scenery is not the best way to work in local colour; it is liable to become guide-booky. Neither is a catalogue of the beauty spots of a locality any better. Usually the most advantageous method is a judicious, illuminating touch here and there, revealing outstanding characteristics, and emphasising the material things that give "colour," *i.e.*, variety and vivid distinction, to a scene.

They may be topographical characteristics or they may be personal characteristics.

Beginners think that local colour is primarily a matter of hills and hedgerows, sunbonnets and smocks—the picturesque element that we look for in the countryside. But conversation can give local colour to a story without a single descriptive sentence. Pett Ridge can transport you in an instant to the heart of Hoxton or the Walworth Road, by means of some bit of cockney dialect. W. W. Jacobs will give a salty, far-sea-faring flavour to the most untravelled public-house in Poplar, in merely recounting a trifling difference of opinion between some of the customers!

Local colour has justified the existence of more than one book that is thin both in literary quality and in plot; *The Lady of the Lake* is an instance. But I do not advocate a writer aiming for success on similar lines.

Some words and expressions open up a much wider vista to the mind's eye than do others. Consider your descriptive passages critically, and see if, by a different choice of words, you can, in the same length of sentence, give the reader a larger outlook.

American Writers excel in the Handling of Local Colour

Some British writers appreciate to the full the artistic value of local colour (Rudyard Kipling and Mrs. F. A. Steel can make one feel as well as see India; Blackmore's books breathe Devonshire; Lafcadio Hearn—if one can call him British!—envelops one in the Oriental odour of Japanese temples; Shan F. Bullock's stories are Ireland herself); but many ignore its possibilities and set the scene with a nondescript society background, or an equally non-commital rural haze.

American writers make rather more use of local colour. And the reason is clear: no other country presents so great a variety in the way of climate, scenery, and human types as does the United States. An American author need only sit down and write of what he sees immediately around him, and, so long as he keeps away from such modern items as the ubiquitous commercial traveller and advertisement signs, and devotes his attention to natural objects and local paraphernalia (human and otherwise), he is certain to be recording what is novelty to a large proportion of his fellow-countrymen. Moreover Americans are more given to dealing with things in a straightforward, unconventional manner than are the British writers, writing of what they actually know and see around them, unhampered by classical traditions and age-old literary usages. Hence, there is often a freshness, a vividly-alive quality in their descriptions, that can only be obtained by writing with a subject red-hot in the mind.

The author who merely rushes into the country for a few days, or spends a couple of weeks on the Continent, or sprints through the European ports of China, to obtain local colour, for a story, usually gets about as "stagey" and artificial a result as does the home-keeping, middle-class girl, who has her heroine presented at the Court of St. James, and draws the local colour from the Society columns of a daily paper!

You must know your "locality" well yourself if you are to make the local colour real to your readers; second-hand or hastily collected data are no good.

The would-be author will do well to study typically-American authors, with a view to observing their use of local colour—particularly those who wrote some of their best work before the motor-car and telephone exercised their levelling and linking-up influences.

To name one or two: Mary E. Wilkins and Sarah Orne Jewett have specialised on New England village life; Charles Egbert Craddock (Miss Murfree) on the Great Smoky Mountains of Tennessee; George Cable on Louisiana; James Lane Allen on Kentucky; Amélie Rives, in her earlier books, on Virginia; etc.

And it is worth while noting that such writers give, not only pictures of the scenery about them, but also an insight into the native character. Thus both Mary E. Wilkins and Sarah Orne Jewett depicted the rigid pride of the New Englanders, as well as the poor but picturesque quality of the soil. George Cable showed the temperament of the Southerner as well as the tropical glamour of the Southern States. Owen Wister has made us love the large-hearted, child-like, primitive cowboy, as well as feel the vastness and the very air of the plains and the mountains of Wyoming.

Such work is local colour at its best, since it gives us the human traits as well as the scenic conditions predominating in a locality, and enables us to form a mental picture of the people and the place as a whole.

Closely allied to this, is that most fascinating study—the effect of climate, scenery, and general environment on character. But as that subject is outside the purview of this book, I merely suggest it to the student as something well worth following up, if there be an opportunity for first-hand observation.

For the novelist who specialises on temperamental delineation, it has wide possibilities.

CREATING ATMOSPHERE

Have you ever seen a landscape painting that was one expanse of correctness in detail, and yet seemed either utterly dead, or to walk out of the canvas at every point and hit you violently in the eye? Such a painting often has a bright-red tiled roof—every tile visible and in its proper place; a violently blue sky decorated here and there with solid masses of apparently unmeltable snow; grass an acute green; trees emphatic as to outline, every branch clearly defined in its appointed place; sheep standing out like pure-white snowflakes on the acute grass; the smoke from the cottage chimney a thick grey mass suggesting a heavy bale of wool; each brick, each window frame, each paling emphasised with careful exactness.

The amateur who produces a painting after this style is usually very pleased with it, and attributes any adverse criticism, that a competent artist may pass upon it, to professional jealousy!

"What is wrong with it?" I have heard a student ask, when a master has condemned such a canvas. "It was all there, every detail, exactly as I have painted it."

Yes, it may have been all there, but something else was there which the artist omitted to include, and the something else was "atmosphere." The artist may put in every twig and tile, every plant and pane of glass; but if he omit the play of light, the glamour of haze, the mystery of shadow, the marvellous suggestiveness of the undefined, his painting will be lifeless and wooden, or altogether unbalanced, no matter how accurate the drawing.

Equally, the author needs atmosphere if his writing is to rise above the dead level of the uninspired; but while one can define to some extent (though not entirely) what is atmosphere in a painting, it is next to impossible to give an exact definition of atmosphere in writing. It is an elusive quality difficult to describe off-hand. So intangible is it that you can seldom put your finger on a passage and say, "Here it is!" yet all the while you may be fully conscious of there being—back of the writing—something more than plot, or purpose.

The atmosphere of a book may appertain to matters moral or material; it may affect the mind or the emotions; it may be beneficial or baneful; it may give colour or glamour, light or shade; it may be mysterious or mesmeric. But whatever its trend, in the main it lies in suggestiveness rather than in definite statement. Like its prototype, "atmosphere" in writing is an unseen environment, yet it permeates and influences the whole, giving it character and even vitality.

"ATMOSPHERE" IS INVALUABLE AS A TIME SAVER

In writing it is possible to suggest a great deal that could not be described in detail within the limits imposed on you by the length of your book and the consideration of balance. Moreover, the things suggested may be of secondary importance beside the main action of the story, and yet be very useful in furthering the idea you have in mind, or in helping to convey a particular impression.

In such cases the introduction of atmosphere may do much for you. While you give only a hint here and there, or a few sidelights in passing, you may yet manage to convey to the readers a "feeling" that carries them beyond the cut-and-dried facts you may be handling, or lifts them above the mere working-out of a plot. It is the haze that may hide, and yet indicate, a something in the distance, just beyond the range of sight—and the suggestion of something still beyond is always alluring; the infinite within us rebels against finite limitations, and welcomes anything that points to further ideas, further possibilities.

Thus atmosphere is invaluable as a time saver. Life is too short (and the publisher too chary of his paper and printing bill) to allow any of us, save the truly famous, to describe minutely the whole background of our writing, spiritual, mental, or material. If we can, by a few expressive words, or phrases, create an atmosphere that shall reproduce in the reader's mind the train of thought, or the scene, that was in our own mind as we wrote, we shall, obviously, be spared the making of many sentences, and the covering of much paper with descriptive matter and soul analyses, that might otherwise overweight our main theme.

Abstract Qualities are Usually Suggested

Atmosphere usually suggests some abstract quality rather than a concrete item. We say that a work has an outdoor atmosphere or an old-world atmosphere or a healthy atmosphere; or we may merely say "it has atmosphere," meaning a subtle over- (or under-) current that clothes the framework of the narrative with a glamour or a spiritual quality that will help to reinforce, or mellow, or illuminate the author's picture. But we do not say a book has a millionaire atmosphere, or a detective atmosphere, even though the book be about these people. They correspond with the solid objects in the landscape, and are quite distinct from the atmospheric effects that can do so much to enhance the charm, or subdue the sordidness, of these solid objects.

It does not necessarily follow that the atmosphere of a book is a wholesome one. There are some writers who create a positively poisonous atmosphere for the mind; but, fortunately, the trend of humanity is in the direction of clean thought and wholesome living, even though our progress be slow and we encounter setbacks; and vicious books are seldom long-livers, while those the public call for again and again are invariably books with a healthy atmosphere.

The student might make a special note of this!

Atmosphere in a well-written book is often so unobtrusive that the reader fails to recognise it as a specific element in the make-up of the story that did not get there by accident. It is so easy to fall into the error of thinking that this or that characteristic or ingredient is due to the author's style, or temperament, or genius; certainly it may be due to either or all of these things, but if it is worth anything it is also due to a well-thought-out scheme on the part of the writer.

In other words, atmosphere only gets into a work if it is put there. It does not merely "happen along," and if you want your writing to be imbued with atmosphere, you must supply it; it won't come of itself. And before you can supply it, you must first think out what you want that atmosphere to be and then decide how best you can secure it.

"ATMOSPHERE" COVERS A WIDE RANGE OF SUGGESTION

It may have to do with spiritual aspects of life—high ideals, faith, healthy thought, right living. Ruskin's *Sesame and Lilies* comes under this head, even though the subject-matter is not religious according to our ordinary use of the word. From beginning to end one is thinking on a higher plane than that of material consideration; one's thoughts are continually branching out beyond the actual purport of the book as set forth by the author.

An old-world atmosphere has a special charm for many readers. We find it in *Cranford*, Jane Austen's books, and many others of a bygone period—though it should be noticed that in these cases the authors did not purposely incorporate it in their work. They put atmosphere, certainly; but it has only become an "old-world" atmosphere by the courtesy of Father Time: in their own day, these books were quite up-to-date productions. Certain modern books have an old-world atmosphere—*The Broad Highway* and *Our Admirable Betty*, by Jeffery Farnol; *When Knighthood was in Flower*, by Charles Major (and many others will occur to the mind); but in each case the old-world atmosphere had to be put there very carefully by the author.

The hysterical atmosphere needs no description. We know too well the type of book that keeps its characters (and aims to keep its readers), from the first chapter to the last, keyed up to an unnatural pitch of emotionalism, with copious details about everybody's soulful feelings and temperaments and lingerie. Books with this atmosphere were constantly striving to get their heads above water in the years of this century preceding the war. They are interesting from one, and only one, point of view: they indicate the diseased mentality that has always come to the surface in periods of the world's history prior to some great human upheaval.

A pessimistic atmosphere is fairly common—especially does it seem to find favour with young writers. One of the best examples of a book with a really pessimistic atmosphere is the *Rubáiyát* of Omar Khayyám.

Atmosphere has sometimes transformed the commonplace into something rare and delightful. *Our Village*, by Miss Mitford, is an instance. Here you have the most ordinary of everyday events described in such a way that they are invested with a halo of charm.

TO CREATE AN ATMOSPHERE

To create the atmosphere you desire, you must be thoroughly imbued with it yourself—you cannot manufacture it out of nothing. It must so possess you while you are at your work that it is liable to tinge all you write. You will never make other people sense what you do not sense yourself.

For instance, it would not be possible for an out-and-out pagan to write a book with a sympathetic evangelical atmosphere, any more than the Kaiser could write a book imbued with the spirit of true Democracy.

Then you must insinuate your atmosphere at times and seasons when it will make the most impression on the reader without interfering with, or hindering, the development of the story; remembering that it is always better to suggest the atmosphere than to put it in with heavy strokes.

You may wish to make a story the very breath of the out-doors. But in order to do this, it would not be necessary to stop all the characters in whatever they were saying or doing, while you describe scenery and sunsets, or explain to the reader how "out-doory" everything and everybody is! This would easily spoil the continuity and flow of the whole, by switching the reader's mind off the plot and on to another train of thought. Instead, you would make the whole book out-doory without any pointed explanation—"setting the stage" in the open air as much as possible, emphasising the features of the landscape rather than boudoir decorations, mentioning the sound of the soughing trees or the surging sea, rather than the tune the gramophone was playing; introducing the scent of the larches in the spring sunshine rather than the odour of tuberoses and stephanotis in a ballroom. In each case the one would suggest freedom in the open air, while the other would suggest conventionalities indoors.

In some such way, you would rely on touches in passing to produce the desired effect, always bearing in mind the importance of getting these touches as telling as possible.

Such allusions (often merely hinted at, rather than spoken) should be equal in effectiveness to long paragraphs of detailed description; therefore, choose carefully the means by which you hope to secure your end. Your touches must be so true and so sure that they instantly convey to the reader's mind your own mental atmosphere.

In this, as much as in any other phase of writing, you need an instinct for the essentials, i.e. a feeling that tells you instantly what will contribute most surely to the making of the atmosphere you desire, and what is relatively unimportant.

Atmosphere is the element in your work that can least of all be faked without detection—or cribbed from other writers.

It must permeate the whole of your story whether long or short, and be something beyond the mere words you write down. The readers must feel, when they finally close the book, that they have got more from you than what you actually said; that you led their thoughts in directions that carried them off the highway of the obvious, giving them visions of things that were unrecorded.

THE METHOD OF PRESENTING A STORY

The method of presenting the story needs a little consideration.

The most common, and the most desirable as a rule, is the narrative, told in a third person; i.e. the writer relates a story about certain people, but does not himself pose as a character involved in the story. Beginners will do well to adhere to this type of story, until they have attained to a certain amount of fluency with their ideas.

Writing in the First Person

Another popular method is the narrative told in the first person, *i.e.* the writer relates a story about certain people, in which he also plays a more or less important part. If well written, this form makes a pleasant change from the story written in the third person; but it necessitates a certain amount of experience on the part of the writer, if it is to be saved from dullness.

Moreover, its limitations are hampering to the beginner. If you are writing in the third person, you, as the author, are allowed (by that special concession granted to makers of fiction) to know everything that every character in your story thinks or does. You may relate in one paragraph what the hero was thinking and doing in San Francisco, and in the next what the heroine was thinking and doing at the same moment in New York.

But if you are writing in the first person, you have not the same licence to roam all over the universe, penetrating the deepest recesses of people's lives and laying bare their secret thoughts to the glare of day. You are supposed to stick to your own part and mind your own business. If you manage to find out other people's business as the story proceeds, there must be some sort of circumstantial evidence as to how you found it out; it will not be enough merely to state that it is so, as you could do were you writing in the third person.

For instance, in a Ms. I pick up from the pile on my table I read:

> "He paused when he reached the drawing-room door and glared at her, livid with rage. She returned his look with one of haughty indifference. Then he left the house, and as he walked along the cheerless streets, he clenched his fists and hissed between his teeth, 'You shall suffer for this.' She, meanwhile, rang the bell for tea and resumed the novel upon which she had been engaged when he arrived."

Told in the third person, it is easy to let the reader know what he and she were thinking and saying and doing at the same moment. But supposing you were writing all this in the first person with yourself as the heroine, it would not be so easy to convey the same information to the reader. You could write:

> "He paused when he reached the drawing-door and glared at me, livid with rage. I returned his look with one of haughty indifference. Then he left the house, and I rang the bell for tea and resumed the novel upon which I had been engaged when he arrived."

But if you wished to let the reader know how the bad-tempered creature clenched and hissed, you would have to get at it by some round-about means—your dearest friend might call at the moment and tell you that she had just passed him in the cheerless street clenching and hissing; or some other such device could be employed. But all this involves extra thought and care in the construction of the story.

A STUMBLING-BLOCK TO THE AMATEUR

Amateurs are much given to story-writing in the first person; it seems such an easy method (when they know nothing about it); they invariably see themselves in a leading part, and make the hero or heroine do and be all they themselves would like to do and be. But they never go far before they trip up against this block of stumbling—the impossibility of the first person singular "I" being in two places at the same time, and seeing inside people's hearts and brains, to say nothing of their locked cupboards and secret drawers.

Also, the beginner is apt to forget the *rôle* he is supposed to be playing when he puts himself into a story, and he lapses, at intervals, into the third person.

Sometimes, in order to dodge the difficulties, an author will write one part in the form of a diary, thus enabling a character to talk about herself (it is usually a feminine character who keeps a diary!). Then, when the limitations of the first person singular hamper the progress of the story, the diary is dropped for a time, while the author revels in the all-embracing freedom of writing in the third person.

This is a weak method, however, and plainly a subterfuge; being practically an announcement that the author could not or would not take the trouble to work the story through in correct form. It is also bad from an artistic standpoint; it does not hang together well; past and present tenses are apt to get mixed; it produces an unsatisfactory feeling in the mind of the reader, who so often is in doubt as to whether the author is writing as a character in the story or merely as the author—and anything that leaves a confused, unsatisfactory feeling in the reader's mind is poor art.

WRITING A STORY IN THE FORM OF A DIARY

A story written entirely in the form of a diary is sometimes attempted. And closely allied to this is the story written as a series of letters.

Both methods are popular with amateurs. Most people regard a diary as the simplest type of writing, requiring neither style nor sequence, nor even the thinnest thread of connection running through the whole, unless the author so desires. Moreover, though every one does not feel competent to write a book or even a short story, we all feel competent to keep a diary—most of us *have* kept one at some time in our career. What can be easier therefore than to write a story in diary form? And we proceed to write our story as we wrote our own diary, with this difference that we put into the fiction diary the sort of happenings we used to deplore the lack of, when we wrote down our own daily experiences.

Until we have given some study to the subject we do not recognise that, while a series of somewhat disconnected sentences and brief entries may be very useful as records for future reference, likewise may be moderately serviceable as safety-valves for overwrought, self-centred temperaments, they are seldom of interest to any one save the writer, and if put forward as recreational reading, may easily prove uninteresting in the extreme, even with the addition of a love episode! A story in diary form needs to be written by an experienced pen if it is to resemble a genuine diary, and yet hold the reader's interest throughout, and culminate in a good climax.

A Story told in Letters

A story told in a series of letters can easily be the dullest thing imaginable. What is an excellent letter seldom makes an excellent chapter in a novel. A letter, if it is to seem a real letter, should be discursive; and this is the very thing the amateur needs to guard against when writing a story, if that story is to show force and action; he is prone to be too discursive as it is. In any case, unless it is remarkably well done, the reader chafes at the delay inevitably caused by the irrelevant small talk that is the hallmark of most letters.

Some writers have managed to handle the "letter-form" in an interesting manner, by relying on descriptive narrative, rather than any striking plot, to hold the reader. *The Lady of the Decoration* by Frances Little, is a good example.

The Introduction of Dialect

Dialect should be approached with caution. It is so easy to be tedious and unintelligible in this direction.

Remember that you are writing in what is almost a fresh language to most people, when you employ a dialect that is purely local; hence you are imposing an extra mental strain on the reader; and in order to compensate for the additional demand you make on his brain, you must give him something above the average in interest. No one, in these days of hustle, is going to take the trouble to wade through a species of unknown tongue, and wrestle with weird spelling and unfamiliar idiom, unless there is something remarkably worth while to be got out of it. And for one who will spare the time to fathom the mysteries of the dialect, there are thousands who will give it up.

The Object Of Writing a Book is not to Befog the Reader's Mind

If it be necessary to write in a particular dialect, avoid so far as possible the use of expressions that in no way explain themselves, and crowding the pages with the more obscure colloquialisms of the district. The object of writing a book is not to befog the reader's mind.

One knows that dialect is sometimes imperative in order to create the right atmosphere and to state things as they actually occurred. In such cases it is usually best to use it only in small quantities—as where a native strolls across very few pages, and is on view for only a short while. Yet you must see that your dialect is correct. Merely to write a few words phonetically, and put a "z" in place of an "s" (as is sometimes done, for instance, when making a native of Somerset speak), is not convincing.

To write a story throughout in dialect calls for exceptional skill; and, as a rule, it can only be done successfully by those who have known a dialect from childhood, or at any rate have spent some years in its company. The names of Sir James Barrie and S. R. Crockett naturally come to one's mind in this connection.

"AN HONEST TALE SPEEDS BEST BEING PLAINLY TOLD"

The beginner will be wise to write his early experiments in plain English and in the third person. Fiction that is free from confusion of style, mixed methods, and uncertainty of handling always does the best. The story that is related in a clear direct manner is most popular with the public—likewise, it is the most difficult to write well, though few beginners believe this: it looks so very simple!

FALLACIES IN FICTION

I have come to the conclusion that the contrariness of human nature is largely responsible for the rejection of many of the Mss. that never get into print; but not the contrariness of the editor (as the unsuccessful writer generally thinks when he sees his Ms. back once more in the bosom of his family).

Most of us, at one period or another, feel we could shine much more brilliantly in some other environment than the one in which we find ourselves. It has been described as "a divine discontent." There is plenty of discontent about it, I allow; but I am not so sure that it is divine. While it may be, and often is, the expression of a real need for a little more growing space, it is sometimes the outcome of mere restlessness, or a lazy, selfish desire to escape the irksome things that are in our own surroundings, vainly imagining that we can find some pathway in life where there are no disagreeables to be faced.

But whatever the motive may be, there is a universal idea among the inexperienced that some other person's job is preferable to their own; some one else's circumstances more interesting and romantic and dramatic and enthralling than theirs could ever be. And the result is—much wasted opportunity.

THE AMATEUR SO SELDOM HAS FIRST-HAND KNOWLEDGE OF HIS SUBJECT

Now the sum-total of this, in regard to story-writing, is the fact that fully 80 per cent. of the fiction submitted to editors deals with situations of which the writer has practically no first-hand knowledge; as a natural consequence it is unconvincing and often incorrect.

The schoolgirl who has never travelled beyond Folkestone or Boulogne, and whose knowledge of fearsome weapons is limited to a hockey-stick, riots one across the Continent on a "Prisoner of Zenda" chase, directly she starts to write.

The girl of twenty, living a quiet, useful life in some small provincial town, in close attendance upon a kindly invalid aunt, devotes the secret midnight candle to writing the life-story of a heartless butterfly of a faithless wife: while the kindly invalid aunt is surreptitiously writing decorous mid-Victorian stories of very, *very* mild wickedness coming to a politely bad end, and oppressively good virtue arriving at the top (with more moral advice than plot, or anything else). The niece imagines she is writing just the type of story that the public craves; and the aunt is under the delusion that hers is just the sort of literature that is wanted for distribution among factory girls.

The maiden of high degree writes of the lily-white beauty of the girl in the grimy garret. The democratic daughter of the colonies invariably sprinkles a few titles about her Ms.

Before the war, the anæmic young man in a city office, who spent most of the year in a crowded suburb and his short vacation at some crowded seashore resort, persistently wrote of the exploits of a marvellous detective who ran Sleuth-hound Bill to earth in Gory Gulch. Since 1914, he (the young man) has sent me many Mss.—from France, Salonika, Egypt, India, and Flanders—and these are generally love stories, and seldom bear a trace of battle-smoke or high adventure. (I am speaking of amateur work, remember.)

I have nothing to say against a desire for new horizons; it is a legitimate part of our development. And I can understand that for a certain type of weakly and rather starved personality there is a slight compensation for the lack of change they crave, in putting down on paper their longings and ideals, and in writing romance in which they secretly see themselves in the leading part.

But this is not saleable matter; neither is it particularly readable matter, as a general rule (though there are occasional exceptions, of course). Because in such cases the writers are invariably dealing with situations the inwardness of which they know really nothing. Or else all their knowledge has been obtained from the writings of others; they are merely repeating other people's ideas and other people's descriptions.

Choose your Topic from your own Environment

You cannot write convincingly on topics about which you know little. You can cover reams of paper—amateurs are doing it every day of the year!—with descriptions of people, and houses, and scenes, and walks of life with which you have only a hearsay acquaintance; but such writing is scarcely likely to be worth printing and paying for.

If the schoolgirl, instead of wasting her time on something that reads like a washed-out *réchauffé* of *The Scarlet Pimpernel*, would try her hand at a story of schoolgirl life, she might produce something really bright and alive, even though it lacked the symmetry and finish that years of practice bring to a writer. And though the Ms. did not find a market at the time, on account of immaturity of style, it might prove valuable later on when the writer had gained experience. It would give her data she had forgotten in the intervening years.

And the girl who spends her ink on the philanderings of the faithless wife (a species, by the way, that she has probably never set eyes on, having been brought up like most of the rest of us in a decent circle of sane relations and friends) might, perhaps, have done some charming pictures of domestic life, as did the authors of *Cranford* and *Little Women* in their day.

If the aunt, instead of hoping to influence factory girls of whom she knows absolutely nothing, and whose conversation, could she but hear it, would be an unintelligible language to her, had turned her invalidism to practical account, and passed on useful hints and ideas to other invalids, she might have written something that would have been welcomed by others similarly handicapped.

And so on, down to the city clerk, who never can be made to realise that a type of story most difficult to lay hands on is the one that deals, accurately, with the inside of that world peopled by the bankers and stockbrokers and money magnates. The detective tracking Sleuth-hound Bill has the tamest walk-over in comparison with the daring, and tense excitement, surrounding some financial deals.

ORIGINAL WORK IS RARE: THE UNIVERSAL TENDENCY IS TO COPY

I do not say that these writers would necessarily have placed their Mss. had they written on the lines suggested; it takes something besides the theme and background to make a good story. But I do say that they would have been many degrees nearer publication, had they dealt with types and circumstances that had come within their personal cognisance, rather than with those they only knew by hearsay.

The outsider would scarcely credit how rare it is for an editor to receive a piece of really original work; the universal tendency is to copy other people's productions rather than trouble to discover original models.

The schoolgirl, studying water-colour drawing, prefers to work from a "copy," showing some other person's painting of a vase of flowers, rather than have her own vase filled with real flowers before her. Some one else's work saves the inexperienced the responsibility of selection—and selection is always a difficult point for the beginner, who finds it hard to decide what to include in, and what to leave out of, a picture.

BEGINNERS ARE SELDOM AWARE THAT THEY ARE COPYING OTHERS

In the same way, inexperienced fiction writers find it easier to copy other people's stories; though, unlike the schoolgirl and her painting-copy, they are quite unconscious that they are doing so; they usually imagine that what they have written is entirely original.

It is difficult to get the novice to distinguish between writing anything down on paper, and creating it in his own brain. So many think the mere passing of thoughts through the brain, and the transmitting of those thoughts to paper, are indications of their ability to write; and that what they write must be original.

And yet in most beginners' Mss. scarcely any of the incidents, or situations, or plots ever came within the writer's own purview; the majority are hashed up from the many stories one reads nowadays—though the author has no idea that he is only stringing together selected ideas that originated in other people's brains.

There are many reasons to account for this. For one thing, the novice feels safe in using the type of material that has already been published. The world is wide, human nature is varied, and it is not easy to decide what to take; therefore the writer who plans his story on time-honoured lines is relieved of the responsibility of selection.

Then, again, if a particular type of story has been accepted and published, it has received a certain hall-mark of approval, and forthwith others tread the same path; there is less uncertainty here than in breaking new ground.

There is yet another reason: to evolve anything that is new and unhackneyed necessitates our taking trouble; and some amateurs will not take any more trouble than they can possibly help; they do not recognise that writing stands for hard work.

Tried Old Friends we have Met before

I cannot spare the space to touch on well-worn plots, but here are a few of the sentences and expressions that haunt amateur Mss.

Have you ever read a story that opened, "It was a glorious day in June," followed by a page of blue sky, balmy breezes, humming bees, not a leaf stirred, and scent of roses heavy on the air? Of course you have. We all have. That glorious day in June is one of the most precious perennials of the story-writer's stock-in-trade.

You know at once that twenty summers will have passed o'er *her* head, and that *he* is just round the corner waiting to come upon her all unawares, so soon as the author can quit cataloguing nature's beauties.

And have you ever read a story that opened with "A dripping November fog enveloped the city"? Of course you have; and you know at once, before you get to the next line, which describes its denseness and the slippery pavements, and a host of other discomforts, that you are going to be ushered into an equally dismal city boarding-house, and introduced to a lovely-complexioned girl whose frail appearance is only enhanced by her deep mourning, and hear the sad story of the pecuniary straits that necessitated her bringing her widowed mother (often fractious), or it may be a younger sister (always sunny and the lodestar of her life), from their lovely old home in the country, while she earned a living in town. And, without fail, she has always imagined that they were well provided for, till the family lawyer (always old) broke the news after the funeral that the place was mortgaged up to the hilt, and even her father's life insurance had been allowed to lapse.

You know all the rest—the dreary tramp round in search of work, and the way she irons out her threadbare garments to make them last as long as they can (irrespective of the fact that the mourning was new only a few weeks before, and she presumably had a good stock of underwear in her prosperous days), and a host of other harrowing experiences until—it comes right in the end.

And all because the story opened with a dripping November fog! Why, I believe the average amateur would consider it almost improper to start a desolate orphan on a quest for work in the metropolis in anything other than a dense November fog!

And yet—how much more cheerful for her, poor dear, could she but begin her career on a dry day—and some November days in London are quite sunny and bright—so much better for her in the thin jacket she always wears on such occasion, and her worn-out shoes!

It would be such a blessed thing if we need not start with the weather, nor the number of summers that had floated over the sweet young heroine's head (or winters, if the central figure be an old man). But the amateur clings to these openings.

Then take "the boudoir." After the weather I don't think anything haunts me more persistently than the boudoir. "Lady Gwennyth was sitting reading a letter in her luxurious (or cosy, or dainty) boudoir, when——" etc.

Now why is it that the girl who starts out to write fiction loves to introduce her heroine in this wise? It is most unlikely that the amateur knows much about a boudoir—few of us do. It is a room that appertains solely to the rich, and to only a small proportion of the rich at that. I know many wealthy women and many well-born women who haven't a boudoir, simply because the cramped conditions of modern living seldom leave them a room to spare for this purpose. The fact is the boudoir proper does not really belong to this purposeful age. It is a relic of the more leisurely Victorian times and the ease-loving, well-to-do Frenchwoman of pre-war days. Most modern women have very little time to spend in a boudoir if even they need one; nevertheless it appears with unfailing regularity in stories dealing with the richer ranks of life, till you would think it was as necessary to a woman's entourage as—an umbrella!

Why is it that the heroine has usually refused a couple (if not more) offers of marriage, before she is brought to our notice, with yet another offer looming on the horizon? In real life, as we know it in this twentieth century, it is most unusual for a girl to be constantly turning down offers of marriage like applications for charity subscriptions though there are exceptions here and there, certainly.

Yet I scarcely open a love-story that does not state that the heroine had already refused "every eligible man in her circle"; though the reader can seldom see why *one* man should have proposed to the damsel, much less a crowd!

The heroine presented to us by the amateur is invariably a most ordinary young person, often quite uninteresting, and lacking the faintest streak of distinctiveness. And then the question arise—Why should all the eligible men in the town have proposed to her?

Perhaps one explanation is the fact that inexperienced writers have not learnt the art of depicting character; as they do not know how to convey an idea of her attractiveness, they think if they state that she was attractive that is sufficient. But statements are not sufficient; she must be attractive.

The youthful heroine and the aged grandmother may also be quoted as evergreen types that long ago had become monotonous. Whether girls married in their teens as a matter of course, a couple of generations ago, I do not know, as I was not there; but the youthful heroine was a *sine quâ non* in Victorian fiction.

She is not a *sine quâ non* now, however; anything but; the seventeen-year-old bride is by no means the rule in these times; there is practically no limit nowadays to the age at which a woman may receive offers of marriage.

Nevertheless, the amateur persistently follows bygone models, and still clings to the very young heroine; no more than eighteen summers are, at the outside, allowed to pass over her lovely head before she is introduced to our notice.

And certain traditions are still followed in regard to other details. Her complexion is always of the rose-petal order, her hair is always escaping in a series of stray curls about her neck and forehead (and, by the way, these "stray curls" of fiction are sadly responsible for many of the untidy lank locks of to-day!). If you read as many Mss. as I do, you would think that no straight-haired, ordinary complexioned girl had the least chance of a personal love-story, despite the fact that most of the girls one knows in real life, who have married and lived "happy ever after," have been either sallow or sunburnt or colourless, or just healthy-looking.

If you doubt whether a successful heroine can be evolved out of a woman no longer in her teens, and with a complexion that would not stand pearls, remember the Hon. Jane, in *The Rosary*.

In addition to the youthful heroine, the aged grandmother needs to be given a long rest. When the young wife who married in her teens visits her old home in company with her one-year-old infant, it is invariably the dearest old lady who comes forward to embrace her first grandchild; and from her own conversation and the description of her general appearance, the sweet old soul must be at least eighty, despite all that Nature might rule to the contrary, to say nothing of the dressmaker!

Tradition has it that grandmothers must have white hair, and spectacles, voluminous skirts, and knitting in their hands as they sit in an easy-chair with comfortably slippered feet on a hassock; and that is the sort of grandmother the amateur brings on the scenes, irrespective of the fact that the grandmother of to-day is skipping about in girlish skirts and high-heeled shoes, with hair and complexion as youthful as she likes to pay for.

Nothing in the way of fiction is more difficult to write than a thoroughly good love story. And yet the beginner invariably starts with a love story, and continues with love-stories, as though there were no other possible selection.

I do not think it is often possible to write a good love-story until one has had some experience of life. It is so easy to mistake neurotic imaginings and over-strung emotionalism for love; and it is still easier to fall back on the conventional things that the conventional hero and heroine do and say in the conventional novel, and imagine that we are recording our own ideas and experiences.

There are several reasons why the love-story appeals to the girl who is starting out to write. She is looking forward to a love-story of her own, if she be a normal girl, and has already seen herself in the part of her favourite heroine. Naturally it is not surprising that love-stories are of absorbing interest to her. And a girl usually sees herself as the heroine of her own early love-stories; and she invariably makes her heroine do and say what she would like to do and say under the circumstances, and at the same time she makes the hero do and say what she would like her own lover to do and say—but it does not follow that this is true to life; or that her lover would say the things she credits him with in her story. Very few proposals in real life ever resemble the proposals in fiction!

A girl will often introduce her heroine in a picturesque pose against some lovely background of hills, or woods, or garden flowers; and the hero coming upon her suddenly is made to pause, lost in admiration of the exquisite picture she makes. The girl writes this because—unconsciously, perhaps—she sees herself in the part, and likes to think she would make a very attractive picture that would rivet a man's attention.

But it is not true to life. In reality, the average man seldom notices the scenic fittings under such circumstances. He either sees the girl—or he doesn't. Unless he is an artist looking for useful subjects for his pictures, the background is not often seen in conjunction with the girl. I merely give this as an instance of the way amateurs are apt to see themselves in an imaginary part that in reality is at variance with "things as they are"; and their writings become artificial in consequence.

There is another reason why the love-story is the beginner's choice: it calls for so few characters. The simplest ingredients are—a nice, beautiful girl and a strong, manly, deserving masculine. Of course, you can vary the flavour by making them rich or poor, misunderstood, down-trodden, capricious, and what not. And you can amplify it by introducing the bold, bad rival (masculine); the superficial, fascinating butterfly rival (feminine); the irate forbidding parent (*his*, if he is rich and she is poor; *hers*, if he is poor and her mother is ambitious and money-grabbing); the designing mischief-maker (a black-eyed brunette, or a brassy-haired blonde); and a host of other well-worn familiar types. But when all is said and done, you need have but two characters to delineate, if you do not feel equal to more—and there is a distinct save of brain in this!

When you reach the climax in any other than a love-story, you are expected to make the *dénouement* something of a slight surprise at any rate, if no more; and we all know that surprises—slight or otherwise—are not altogether easy to manufacture for purposes of fiction. It is simple work to go on talking and describing and making the people talk—about nothing—for pages and pages; but by no means simple to lead it all up to a definite point of culmination. There must be some sort of point to a story; and that point is the trouble as a rule!

But with a love-story, the amateur thinks he need not worry about hunting for a climax—every one knows what the climax must be. "All you have to do is to bring them along the road of life to a suitable spot where they can fall into each other's arms"—thus the novice argues, and proceeds to do it. Another save of brain wear and tear!

In any other situation the *dramatis personæ* are bound to do at least a little talking, to explain how the thing has worked out, or to let you know how matters finally adjusted themselves. But not so our happy lovers! About the longest sentence he is called upon to construct is, "At last!" as he clasps her to him; while her contribution to the duologue need only be, "Darling!" which she whispers, resting her head on his shoulder. And they need not say even this much: for one very favourite method of conclusion, with inexperienced authors, is to bring the hero and heroine suddenly face to face with some such final sentence as, "What they said need not be recorded here: such words are too sacred to be repeated"—a finale that always annoyed me in my young days!

Amateurs are generally very weak in character-drawing, and nowhere is this more noticeable than in love-stories. There is a time-honoured notion that the chief requisites in the heroine are youth and beauty, as I have already said, while the hero must of equal necessity be clean-cut, manly and masterful. With these ideas already fixed in his head, the novice seldom sees any necessity for character-delineation. He explains that the heroine is lovely and the hero in every way a desirable young man, and leaves it at that; forgetting that the mere statement that she is "winsome," or "wistful," or possessed of "clear grey eyes that are the windows of her soul," does not necessarily make her all these things. In the majority of amateur Mss. the heroine, as she depicts herself by word and deed, is a most colourless, stereotyped nonentity; and by no means the glowing, fascinating thing of originality and beauty that the author's adjectives would have us believe; and the hero is frequently no more animated, no more human, than the elegant dummy in a tailor's window.

This may be taken as a fairly safe ruling: If it be necessary for you to label your characters with their chief characteristics, your writing is unconvincing and weak. Their actions should speak louder than your adjectives.

One of the prominent novelists of to-day—who is clever enough and experienced enough to know better—has a trick of letting some one of his characters make a semi-witty remark; after which he adds, "And everybody laughed." This last should be quite unnecessary. If the remark be sufficiently laugh-at-able, it will be self-evident that people smiled; if it is not sufficiently witty to suggest a laugh to the reader, no amount of ticketing will raise a smile, either in the book or out of it.

The same principle should be applied to the presentation of one's characters. If they are to have anything more than a mere walk-on part, they should very quickly explain themselves. The bald statement that the hero is a fine, manly fellow means nothing in reality. What is important is whether his actions and speech suggest a fine, manly character. If they do not, no amount of descriptive matter on the part of the author will conjure up a fine, manly fellow in the reader's imagination.

SOME RULES FOR STORY-WRITING

In presenting a story it is essential that the reader shall have some idea as to what it is about. To start by keeping the reader roaming along for a page or two among unintelligible remarks, and references to unknown or unexplained events, is to give him strong encouragement to shut up the book without troubling to go any further.

There is something very exasperating about a writer who gives no clue as to who anybody is or what anything is; he is every bit as irritating as the one who goes to the other extreme, and drags the reader through the babyhood and school days of the hero's parents.

These are the opening paragraphs of a Ms. offered to me. It is quite a short story, hence there was every reason why space should not have been wasted on unintelligible preamble.

"It happened in this way: through the lions. No, that isn't exactly right though; the lions didn't really do it, would never have thought of doing such a thing; but if I had not gone to see them, it would never have happened. So, you see, they were to some extent responsible.

"I expect you are saying to yourself, 'What was it that happened?' Well that is what I'm going to write about. But first I must tell you that one of my failings from childhood upwards has been the habit of starting to tell my story right in the very middle; and then I always feel so annoyed when, after I've been chattering away for I don't know how long, people look at me and say, 'Perhaps you will try and be lucid and explain what you are talking about!' It never seems to occur to them that it is they who are so stupid. But I will tell you at once about 'me' and then tell you about 'it.' I'll begin at the very beginning, and try to tell you everything in proper orthodox style."

After much more of this description, it turns out at last that the lions were celebrities at a dinner-party where the narrator met the man she ultimately married.

That was all!

It is foolish to keep the reader dangling in suspense, unless the subsequent revelations are to be sufficiently striking to warrant the suspense. A long explanatory deviation from the actual theme is seldom satisfactory or desirable, in a short story, even when the theme is a big one (unless it be absolutely necessary, in order to elucidate some important detail): but it is inexcusable when the subject is trivial and obvious.

The more "body" there is in your Ms. the more it will stand digressive or dilutive passages; the lighter your main theme, the less can you afford to allow the reader's interest to be dissipated over extraneous matter before you reach the main theme.

Until you are an experienced craftsman, introduce the important characters as early as possible. The reader should know them as long as possible if he is to take a keen personal interest in them.

It is better not to describe your characters more than is necessary for actual identification; they should describe themselves by their actions and conversation, as the story proceeds.

To save the monotony of long descriptive passages, that always hamper the movement of a story, it is often possible to make one of the characters, in the course of conversation, give the information that the author is anxious to convey to the reader. But in order to effect this, do not fall into the error of making a character say things that in real life there would be no reason for his saying. You may want to convey the information to the reader that the heroine's ancestors were eminently respectable; but it would be bad art to make her remark to her own parent (or a relative): "As you know, mother dear, grandfather was a distinguished general."

Beginners imagine that the strength of a story is in direct proportion to the way they crowd together incidents, or multiply their characters. But this entirely depends on the quality of the incidents and the importance of the characters.

The whole is greater than a part—always has been and always will be; and if each individual character is weak, and each episode is feeble, no matter how you may elaborate your story, the whole will be weaker than each part.

It is time-saving, when writing a story, to lay the scene in some locality you know well, even though you change the name and preserve its incognito. It is most useful to have a fixed plan of the streets and lanes and buildings and railway station in your mind when writing.

Try to distinguish between a longing to voice your own pent-up emotions, and a desire to give the world something that you think will interest or instruct them. Three-quarters of the love-stories girls write are merely outlets for their own emotions; and picture what they wish would happen in their own lives—with no thought whatever as to whether the Ms. contains anything likely to interest the outsider.

Short sentences and short paragraphs are usually an advantage in stories as well as in articles; they give crispness and brightness to the whole. Whereas long sentences and long paragraphs are both stodgy to read and uninteresting to look at, (and it must not be forgotten that the look of a page sometimes counts a good deal with the public).

I know that instances can be cited where celebrated people have written long sentences and ungainly paragraphs, and yet have been read. President Wilson, in his most famous Note to Germany, led off with a sentence of one hundred and seventy-one words, while there were only twelve full-stops in the whole message. But President Wilson, at that particular date, scored heavily over every other writer, in that the whole world was eagerly willing to read anything he wrote—even though he had omitted all stops and capital letters!—whereas the majority of us, alas, have to persuade or coax or beguile the public into looking at our words of wisdom, and we have to make the reading as easy for people as we can. Otherwise they will not bother their heads about us!

People were willing to put up with President Wilson's diffuse and "trailing" manner of writing, because at the moment he was the mouthpiece of the inhabitants of the United States. Any one who is the mouthpiece of over ninety millions of people can cease to worry about style—some one is sure to read him no matter how he expresses himself.

But so long as we manage to avoid having positions of such greatness thrust upon us, we shall do well to keep our sentences terse and short, and our Mss. broken up into paragraphs.

THE QUESTION OF POLISH

There is much divergence of opinion as to how far it is desirable to polish one's work. Personally I think it all depends upon the work.

Some authors put down their ideas in a very rough form, and seem unable to realise the possibilities of those ideas and their development, till they see them on paper.

Others are able to think in minute detail before they put a line on paper.

Some people can never leave anything alone, and will tinker with half a dozen fresh proofs (if they can induce the publisher to supply them). Others are more sure of themselves, or disinclined to alter what they have written.

The late Guy Boothby used almost to re-write his stories, after they were set up in type; the margins of most of the slip proofs being so covered with new matter and alterations that they had often to be entirely reset. So expensive did this become, that at last I decided to keep his typed Ms. in a drawer for a week or two, and then send it back to him, asking him to do whatever rewriting was necessary before it was set up.

Of course, writers may alter a good deal in their first Ms., before ever it gets to the publisher; but my experience has been that the author who worries his proof is the one who has previously worried his Ms. (and sometimes his family too)! It is primarily a matter of mind-certainty, combined with the question of temperament.

One thing is undeniable: some writers will polish their Mss. into things of beauty; others will polish all the individuality and life out of theirs. In the latter case, however, I am inclined to think there was not much individuality and life to start with!

So far as the beginner is concerned, my advice is Polish; most of us can stand a good deal of this without losing anything worth keeping, or coming to a bad end!

To get under way, Start where you are

Do not waste time in waiting for something extraordinary or sensational to turn up, in the way of a plot, or you may have to wait a long while. Begin with some everyday happening and invest it with personality.

If you can, avoid making your early Mss. love stories. The *dénouement* of a love story is so obvious: try to write something on less obvious lines; it will be better practice for you.

Study some of the many delightful books that have been written in other than love motifs, yet dealing with events of ordinary life; such as *The Golden Age*, and *Dream Days*, by Kenneth Graham; *A Window in Thrums*, by Sir James Barrie; *The Country of the Pointed Firs*, by Sarah Orne Jewett; *Timothy's Quest*, by Kate Douglas Wiggin.

Genius is shown in the ability to take simple themes, and treat them greatly.

About the Climax

The most important part of a story should be the climax (I use the word climax in its modern sense, meaning the terminal point where all is brought to a conclusion, the *dénouement*, the final catastrophe). The climax must be in the author's mind from the very first sentence, and everything he writes should be with this in view—*i.e.*, his own view, not that of the reader; it must be his aim throughout the story to conceal the climax from the reader till the last moment. Nothing with an obvious solution will hold the reader's interest.

Every piece of writing should have some sort of a conclusive ending—a satisfactory one if possible. Writers sometimes make their fiction terminate in an abrupt, unsatisfactory manner, which is no real finish, and leaves the reader wishing it had not all ended like that, and wondering if there is more to come.

When such defects are pointed out, the amateur invariably replies, "But it must end like that, because that is what actually happened." They forget that the fact a circumstance actually happened is no guarantee that it was worth recording; nor is the circumstance necessarily the symmetrical finish to the story,—and a piece of writing should be symmetrical, and in well-balanced design. You cannot always detach an incident from contingent happenings, and then say it is complete. The larger proportion of our actions are linked with, and interdependent upon, other actions.

Therefore see to it that your story terminates in a satisfactory manner. That which apparently ends in failure to-day, may take a new lease of life to-morrow and prove to be merely a stepping-stone to new developments.

It is not bound to be a happy ending (though if there be a choice, happy endings are by far the best, in a world that has enough of sorrow in its work-a-day life); but it must be an ending leaving a sense of right completion with the reader—the conviction that this is the logical conclusion of the whole.

All great works of art leave behind them a sense of fulfilment, the "something attempted, something done," that is always the desirable finale to the human heart and mind. We hate to be left in a state of never-to-be-satisfied suspension; and we invariably reject and condemn to oblivion the work that deliberately leaves us thus.

Some people have an idea that it is "artistic" to leave a story in a half-finished condition, or with a disappointing ending, or a general feeling of blankness. A few years ago there was a mania for this type of story among small writers: those who were not clever enough to produce originality of idea, and at the same time get their work logical, symmetrical and conclusive, would seize on some miserable, or at any rate uncomfortable, ending—drown one of the lovers the day before the wedding; part husband and wife irrevocably, and possibly kill their only child in a railway accident in the last chapter—anything in fact that would produce what one might call a "never-more" finale. And then a certain section of the public (who really did not like it at all, but feared to say so lest they should appear to be behind the times!) would exclaim, "So artistic!"

Yet it was anything but artistic; three-quarters of the time it was logically and morally bad; logically bad because it was seldom the true and natural conclusion that one would have seen in real life; morally bad because it is actually wrong to manufacture and circulate gloom unnecessarily.

I repeat again I would not imply that all endings must be happy; great tragedies need tragic conclusions; suffering is as much a part of real life as joy; a certain course of action must inevitably lead to a sorrowful ending, and there is no getting away from the unalterable truth, "The wages of sin is death." But the type of story to which I am alluding is seldom great or tragic: it is not even painful; it is more often weak and washy, and ends with unsatisfactory incompletion because the author fancied it was brilliantly original!

Always work steadily towards the climax, speeding up the movement as you near the end. Make big events come closer and closer together, with less detail between, the nearer you are to the conclusion.

Do not anticipate your climax, and get there too soon, and then try to make up the book to the required length by adding on an after-piece.

The climax should be such that it leaves in the reader's mind a sense of absolute fitness, a certainty that it was after all the one right ending—even though it came as a great surprise.

THE USE OF "CURTAINS"

When a story is presented in sections, as in a serial or a play, it is advisable to make each section end—so far as possible—in such a manner that the reader is set longing for the next part. Thus, while the climax is generally the solution of a problem, a "curtain" is usually a problem needing solution (literally, a good place for ringing down the curtain, since the audience will be on tenterhooks to know what happens next).

This arrangement is sound business as well as a good mental policy. It is wise to make an instalment leave some final, incisive mark on the mind of the readers, if there is to be an interval before the story is resumed, otherwise it may be difficult for the public to recollect what went before, and the thread of continuity will be lost.

More than this, an editor, despite the usual backwardness of his intelligence, realises the desirability of securing readers for subsequent issues of his periodical, no less than for the current number. If each instalment of the serial terminate with some mystery unsolved, or some hopeless entanglement needing to be straightened out, or some problem that baffles everybody (most of all the readers), it is much more likely that people will rush to secure the next number to see how things turn out, than if the instalment merely ends with the hero indulging in a tame, lengthy soliloquy on artichokes, and leaves nothing more exciting to be settled than whether these same artichokes shall, or shall not, be cooked for the heroine's lunch.

On more than one occasion I have had readers write protestingly because an instalment of a serial has left off cruelly "just when one was frightfully anxious to know what would happen next!" But that is the very place for an instalment to end: good "curtains" are worth as much to a serial as a good plot; and if a story lack good "curtains," an editor thinks twice before purchasing it for serial publication, even though it has undoubted literary merit and will make a good volume.

Inexperienced writers overlook this necessity for holding the reader's attention from section to section, and sometimes offer an editor serial stories without sufficient backbone or dramatic interest to hold the readers' attention from the first instalment to the second, much less for twelve or more detachments.

Or they crowd several excitements into a couple of chapters, and then run on uneventfully for a dozen or so.

This does not mean that problems must crop up mechanically at stated intervals, and the serial be produced on a mathematical basis of one murder, or mystery to so many words! But it does mean that the author must see to it that his important incidents are fairly distributed throughout the work as a whole, and that each chapter ends at the psychological moment. This gives an editor a chance to break the story at places where the excitement runs highest.

Careful attention to balance will help the writer to get the action fairly distributed. If the Ms. be examined as a whole, with this question of balance in mind, the writer will be able to detect if too much movement has been concentrated in one part, with undue expanses of uneventfulness stretching between.

DICKENS WAS AN ADEPT AT "CURTAINS"

No one knew better than Charles Dickens how to keep the reader on the *qui vive* for the next chapter. Joseph H. Choate says in his Memoirs: "As Dickens' books came out they were eagerly devoured in America. *Dombey and Son* came out in numbers long before the laying of the first Atlantic cable, and several numbers went over in fort-nightly steamers, the most frequent communication of that day. In an early part of the story little Paul was brought to the verge of the grave, the last number to hand leaving him hovering between life and death, and all America was anxious to know his fate. When the next steamer arrived bringing decisive news, the dock was crowded with people. The passengers imagined some great national or international event had happened. But it was only the eager reading public who had hurried down to meet the steamer, and get the first news as to whether little Paul was alive or dead."

The late Dr. S. G. Green has told how, at the day school he attended as a boy, "work was suspended once a month on the publication of the instalment of *Pickwick Papers*, which the head master read aloud to the assembled and eager boys. When Mr. Pickwick was released from the Fleet Prison, a whole holiday was given, to celebrate the event!"

This is the type of serial story an editor yearns for: one that will end with so dramatic a "curtain" each month, that the public suspend all employment in order to secure copies of the following issue, and learn what happened next!

Even the final sentences of an instalment with a good "curtain" can be made to do wonders in whetting the reader's appetite for more. But it is advisable to see how they read in connection with the words that inevitably follow. For instance, there was a lurid serial in a daily paper which ended one day with the words:

"'Cat,' she cried, 'vile, odious, contemptible cat.' To be continued to-morrow."

"But," commented *Punch*, "could she do any better than that even after she *had* slept on it?"

ON MAKING VERSE

Most of us break out into verse at one period of our life. Youth starting out to explore a world that seems teeming with new discoveries, generally tries to voice his emotions in poetry—not because youth has any special aptitude for this form of literature, but because the poet has expressed, as no other writer has done, the hopes and ideals, the craving for romance and the thirst for beauty, that are among the characteristics of our golden years. And youth, wishing to voice his own emotions, naturally selects the literary form in which such emotions have already been enshrined.

Verse-writing is a very useful exercise for the student—as I have already stated in a previous chapter; but until we are fairly advanced, it is well to avoid regarding our efforts too seriously.

To string together certain sets of syllables with rhymes in couples, is an exceedingly simple matter; but to write poetry is the highest and the most difficult form of literary art.

It is hard to convince the beginner that the verses he has put together are not poetry—even though they may be technically correct as to make-up, which is by no means always the case. He is inclined to argue that he has dreamed dreams, and seen visions, and travelled far from the prose of life; what he writes, therefore, must be scintillating with star dust, if with nothing more heavenly.

For the making of poetry, the dreams of youth are valuable; take care of them, they are among the precious things of life, and they vanish with neglect or rough handling; but something more than dreams is needful.

STUDY THE LAWS GOVERNING METRICAL COMPOSITION

If you feel you can best express yourself in verse, make a comprehensive study of the laws governing metrical composition. Such knowledge not only enables you to write in a shapely, orderly, pleasing form, but it may also help you to ascertain what is wrong, when something you have written seems jarring, or halting, or lacking at any point.

To many amateurs, laws and rules suggest a cramping influence; they feel sure they could do far better work if unhampered by any restrictions. In reality, however, the limitations such laws impose are a gain to the poet, since they compel him to sort out his ideas, to differentiate between essentials and non-essentials, to condense his thoughts and measure his words. And if properly carried out, all this should result in the reduction of verbosity to the minimum, and a moderately clear presentation of a subject—it does not always, I know, but it ought to do so.

I am neither enumerating nor discussing these laws in this volume, since excellent books on the subject have been published. I merely wish to point out to the student the necessity for giving the matter attention.

Some people think the fact that the idea embodied in their verse is good and ennobling, should condone weak or faulty workmanship. But, alas! in this callous world it doesn't, as a rule.

The ideal verse is that which presents beautifully a great thought in a small compass.

IDEAS ARE MORE IMPORTANT THAN RHAPSODIES

A poem should centralise on some special thought or idea. Rhapsodies, no matter how intense, do not constitute poetry; every poem, be it ever so short, should suggest some definite train of thought. Haphazard statements or description are no more permissible in a poem than in a novel.

All nonsense verse, even, must have an underlying semblance of a sensible idea, though when you come to analyse it, it may turn out to be the height of absurdity.

MOREOVER THE IDEAS SHOULD BE POETIC

Not only must a poem contain a definite idea, it must be a poetic idea, something that will lift the reader above the prose of life. Try to make him see beauty if you can; and to hear beauty in the music of your words. Poetry should be beautiful and suggest loveliness, whenever possible.

However simple and ordinary the subject of your verse, try to carry the reader beyond superficialities, to the wonderful and the unordinary that so often give glory to life's commonplaces.

Take a well-worn subject like the incoming tide; how many people have been moved to write on this topic!

I could not possibly reckon up the number of times I have seen "ocean's roar" rhyming with "rocky shore." The writer who is nothing more than a versifier is content with a description of the sights and sounds of the beach; but the poet looks further than this. Read Mrs. Meynell's "Song," and you will better understand my meaning when I say that the poet must endeavour to show us, through the substance of things material, the shadow of things spiritual.

SONG

By Alice Meynell

As the unhastening tide doth roll,
Dear and desired, upon the whole
Long shining strand, and floods the caves,
Your love comes filling with happy waves
The open sea-shore of my soul.

But inland from the seaward spaces,
None knows, not even you, the places
Brimmed at your coming, out of sight
—The little solitudes of delight
This tide constrains in dim embraces.

You see the happy shore, wave-rimmed,
But know not of the quiet dimmed
Rivers your coming floods and fills,
The little pools, 'mid happier hills,
My silent rivulets, over-brimmed.

What, I have secrets from you? Yes.
But, O my Sea, your love doth press
And reach in further than you know,
And fill all these; and when you go,
There's loneliness in loneliness.

By Courtesy of
The Walter Scott Publishing Co., Ltd.

AMATEUR VERSE USUALLY FALLS UNDER THESE HEADINGS

Putting on one side religious verse (which one does not wish to dissect too brutally, since one recognises and respects the spirit underlying it, despite its sometimes poor technique), amateur verse usually falls under one of four headings:

1. Lovers' outpourings.
2. Baby prattle.
3. Nature dissertations.
4. Stuff worth reading.

The first of these explains itself, and includes perennial poems entitled "Blue Eyes"; "Parted"; "To Daphne" (or Muriel, or Gladys, or some other equally nice person); "Absence"; "My Lady"; "Twin Souls," etc. In these the following are generally regarded as original and delightful rhymes: Love and dove; mourn and forlorn; girl and curl; moon and June; eyes and skies.

Without wishing to hurt any sensitive feelings, truth compels me to state that it is rare for such productions to have any literary value.

The verses coming under the second heading are frequently written by young girls, unmarried aunts, and very new fathers; occasionally mothers give vent to their maternal affection in this way, but more often they find their time fully occupied in attending to the little ones' material needs.

Such poems (often entitled "Lullaby") are usually characterised by an entire lack of anything that could possibly be called an idea. They will apostrophise the infant, and tell it how lovely it is, begging it to go to sleep, and assuring it that mother will keep watch the while—which no up-to-date mother would dream of doing in these busy, servantless days! But as to any concrete reason why the verses were penned, one looks for it in vain.

I do not think such effusions serve any useful purpose. They are not even desirable as an outlet for the feelings, since there are better ways in which one can work out one's affection for a child—woolly boots, pinafores, personal attention, and the like. Nevertheless every woman's paper is deluged with Mss. of this type.

The Nature dissertation is a trifle better than the preceding, because it does offer a little scope for looking around and noting things. But the weakness here is this: the writers do not always look around; they as often sit at a comfortable writing-table indoors and amalgamate other people's observations; and the outcome is a recital of the obvious, with oft-repeated platitudes.

The following are well-worn titles: "A Spring Song"; "Bluebells"; "Twilight Calm"; "Sunset"; "Autumn Leaves"; occasionally they take a Wordsworthian turn, "Lines written on the shore at Atlantic City" or "Thoughts on seeing Stratford-on-Avon for the first time" (such a poem naturally beginning "Immortal Bard, who—" etc.).

At best, the majority of nature poems, as written by the untrained, contain little beyond descriptive passages. This again results in a pointless production that seldom embodies any idea worth the space devoted to it.

You may record the fact that the sun is setting in a blaze of colour; but there is nothing sufficiently remarkable about this to warrant its publication: most people know that the sun occasionally sets in this fashion. If the beauty of the sunset affected you strongly, lifting you above earthly things, and giving you a vision—dim perhaps, but nevertheless a vision—of the Glory that shall be revealed, then it is for you so to describe the beauty of the sunset that you convey to your readers the same feelings, the same uplifted sense, the same vision of the yet greater Glory that is to be. When you can do this, the chances are that you will be writing poetry. But until you can do this, you may be writing nothing better than fragments of a rhyming guide-book.

You may argue that not only did you feel an uplift when you gazed on the sunset, but you re-experience it as you read the poem you wrote upon it.

YOU SEE THE SCENE YOU ARE DESCRIBING: THE READER DOES NOT

Possibly so; because to you the lines conjure up the whole scene; i.e. they serve to remind you of much that is not written down. One word may be enough to recall to your mind the overwhelming grandeur of the sundown in every detail; but it will not be sufficient to spread it out before the eyes of those who did not see the actual occurrence; neither will it reveal to them the uplift of the moment.

The novice so often forgets that his own mind fills in the details of what he has seen, and makes a perfect picture out of an imperfect description. But the reader cannot do this; he has nothing to help him beyond the written words. Therefore the writer must take care to omit nothing that is essential, nothing that will enforce the mental and spiritual conception of a scene. And in order to do this, he must analyse the scene, and ascertain (if he can) what it was that aroused such deep emotion within him. If he can tabulate these items (sometimes it is possible to do so, sometimes it is not), then he must give them special emphasis in his description, no matter what else is omitted.

Whether you are writing descriptive matter in verse or prose, it is well to bear in mind that memory helps *you* to visualise the whole scene, whereas the reader will have no such additional aid.

Poetry should Voice Worldwide, rather than Individual, Need

The primary object of the beginner, in writing verse, is often to voice his own heart's longing; whereas, if his verse is to be of interest to others besides himself, it must voice the longings of other people. Poetry of the "longing" kind should touch on world-wide human need, not merely on an individual want, if it is to waken response in the reader. Of course the individual want may be a world-wide human need: it very often is; but it is not wise to trust to chance in this particular.

Look about you, and see if your experiences are likely to be those of your fellow-creatures. If so, there is more probability that your work will appeal to others than if you take no count of their requirements and centre on your own.

The poet, among other qualifications, has the ability to recognise what humanity wants to say but cannot, and is able to set it down in black and white, so that when the world reads it, it exclaims: "Why, that is just what I think and feel! Only I could never put it into words!"

When Elizabeth Barrett Browning wrote the "Sonnets from the Portuguese," she was writing of her own love for one particular man. So far she was dealing with her own experiences; and if that had been all, the matter might have ended there. But because uncountable women in every land have loved in that same way, have thought those thoughts, and experienced those identical emotions, though they were not able to write of them as Mrs. Browning did, her "Sonnets" found an echo in hearts the world over: they voiced a great human experience, a universal human longing.

The So-called "New Poetry"

One modern phase of verse-making has had a very demoralising effect on the amateur. I refer to the outbreak of shapeless productions—devoid of music, beauty, rhythm, and balance, and often lacking the rudiments of sense—that developed before the war, and has been with us ever since.

The followers of this cult advocate the abolition of all law and order: each goes gaily on his own way, writing whatsoever he pleases, no matter how crude, or banal, or incoherent, or loathsome; lines any and every length; unlimited full stops, or none at all; just what is in his brain—and what a state of brain it reveals! This so-called "new poetry" resembles nothing in the world so much as the Mss. an editor occasionally receives from inmates of lunatic asylums!

Literary effusions of this type are on a par with the cubist and futurist monstrosities that have tried to imagine themselves a new form of pictorial art.

Unfortunately, the desire to kick over all laws and rules, and everything that betokens restraint and discipline, is no new one. Periodically the world has seemed to be attacked with wholesale madness, as history shows; and a pronounced feature of each upheaval has been the attempt of certain deranged imaginations to abolish that order which is Heaven's first law (and which cannot be abolished without wide-spread ruin), and in its place to exalt the deification of self. The years preceding every outbreak have invariably been marked by excesses, licence and extravagance of all kinds; while real art, wholesome living, serious thinking, and steady, well-regulated work, have been at a discount.

Do not be misled by high-sounding statements, that all the incoherency and carelessness and indifferent workmanship exhibited in recent travesties of Art was a groping after better things, the breaking of shackles that chained the free heaven-born spirit of man to miserable mundane convention.

It was nothing of the sort.

Rather, it was a form of hysteria that was the outcome of the "soft" living, the feverish quest of pleasure, the craving for notoriety at the least expenditure of effort, the longing to be perpetually in the limelight, and the absence of self-discipline that was all too noticeable in the earlier years of this century.

The Limitations of Youth

By Eugene Field

I'd like to be a cowboy an' ride a fiery hoss
    Way out into the big and boundless West;
I'd kill the bears an' catamounts an' wolves I come across,
An' I'd pluck the bald-head eagle from his nest!
      With my pistols at my side,
      I would roam the prarers wide,
An' to scalp the savage Injun in his wigwam would I ride—
    If I darst; but I darsen't!

I'd like to go to Afriky an' hunt the lions there,
    An' the biggest ollyfunts you ever saw!
I would track the fierce gorilla to his equatorial lair,
An' beard the cannybull that eats folks raw!
      I'd chase the pizen snakes,
      An' the 'pottimus that makes
His nest down at the bottom of unfathomable lakes—
    If I darst; but I darsen't!

The "new" poetry was a manifestation of the decadence undermining pre-war Art.

Do not be deluded into thinking that the aberrations of ill-trained minds that sometimes flaunt themselves before your bewildered eyes, in some very "thin" volume of verse, or in some freakish periodical, are art, or even worth the paper they are printed on. They are not. Very probably they would never have got into print at all, but for the fact that those who affect the cult are, for the most part, people with more money than discrimination, who can afford to pay for publicity.

Just as a certain type of eccentricity of action may be the precursor of mental disease, so a certain type of eccentricity of thought may be the forerunner of moral and spiritual disease.

Avoid unnecessary abbreviations: *th'* for the, *o'* for of, and similar curtailments. These are often mere mannerisms, and introduced with the idea that they are distinctive: but they are not.

SOME GENERAL HINTS WORTH NOTING

Long lines are better for descriptive verse than short ones.

A stately metre, with well-marked cadence, is best suited to a lofty theme. This is illustrated in "The Valley Song," by the late Mable Earle, which we reprint by courtesy of the *American Sunday School Times*.

A VALLEY SONG

By Mable Earle

"*Because the Syrians have said, The Lord is God of
the hills, but He is not God of the valleys.*"

God of the heights where men walk free,
    Above life's lure, beyond death's sting;
Lord of all souls that rise to Thee,
    White with supreme self-offering;
Thou who hast crowned the hearts that dare,
    Thou who hast nerved the hands to do,
God of the heights! give us to share
    Thy kingdom in the valleys too.

Our eyes look up to those who stand
    Vicegerents of Thy stainless sway,
Heroes and saints at Thy right hand,
    Thy priests and kings of glory they.
Not ours to tread the path they trod,
    Splendid and sharp, still reaching higher;
Not ours to lay before our God
    The crowns they snatched from flood and fire.

Yet through the daily, dazing toil,
   The crowding tasks of hand and brain,
Keep pure our lips, Lord Christ, from soil,
   Keep pure our lives from sordid gain.
Come to the level of our days,
   The lowly hours of dust and din,
And in the valley-lands upraise
   Thy kingdom over self and sin.

Not ours the dawn-lit heights; and yet
   Up to the hills where men walk free
We lift our eyes, lest faith forget
   The Light which lighted them to Thee.
God of all heroes, ours and Thine,
   God of all toilers! keep us true,
Till Love's eternal glory shine
   In sunrise on the valleys too.

Short lines, irregular metre and unusual construction, are best for light or whimsical subjects. "The Limitations of Youth," by Eugene Field, is an example.

To put it another way: when the subject is dignified, the lines should roll along; when the subject is light and airy, the lines should ripple past.

The more peaceful the subject, the more need for mellifluent treatment.

Stern or tragic subjects can stand rugged wording and shape.

Verses written for children, or on childish themes, should be simple in construction, with rhymes near together, and lines of not more than eight syllables as a rule. 8.6's, rhyming alternately, are the easiest to memorise, and therefore the most popular with children.

Examine the poems in Stevenson's *A Child's Garden of Verses*, and note the simplicity of their construction, the music of their rhymes, and their clear, direct method of statement—the latter an essential if children are to be interested.

One of the reasons for the appeal that "Hiawatha" makes invariably to children is its direct form of statement, with few involved sentences; and its eight-syllable lines.

Eugene Field's poems on childhood themes, and some of the passages in "The Forest of Wild Thyme," by Alfred Noyes, are delightful examples of the possibilities of 8.6 lines with alternate rhymes.

Merely to break up prose into lines of irregular length, is not to produce poetry.

There must not only be beauty in individual lines and phrases, but there must be beauty of idea and form in the verses as a whole.

At the same time, never sacrifice sense to sound.

Young writers sometimes say to me, "I see so much, and feel so much, yet

I cannot put it into words: the thoughts are beautiful while they are inside my brain, but there seem no words adequate to express them; I am baffled directly I try to put them down on paper."

Don't despair. Every poet has felt the same: but let it encourage you to recollect that many have got the better of the feeling, by hard work and sheer determination. After all you have all the words there are, and the most famous of poets had no more than this to work with. We sometimes forget that in the end, the greatest writer that ever lived had to reduce everything to the same words you and I are free to use.

You may remember that Mark Twain once went to a well-known preacher, who had delivered a magnificent sermon, and, after extolling it and thanking him for it, the humourist added, "But I have seen every word of it before, in print!"

The astonished preacher asked, indignantly, "Where?"

"In the dictionary," replied Mark Twain.

THE FUNCTION OF THE BLUE PENCIL

Just as we all know that a king would be no king without a crown, and the Lord Mayor of London would be but a mere mortal man without his mace and his gorgeous gilt coach, so no self-respecting editor is supposed to exist apart from a blue pencil. And I admit it is a serviceable article, but, personally, I prefer that it should be used by the contributor. I do not want to have to spend time in revising a Ms., to get it into publishable shape; neither does any other editor.

The blue pencil stands for deletion. Practically every writer needs to cut down the first draft of a story or article. Some prune more severely than others, but all experienced workers reduce and condense before they finally pass a Ms. for publication.

It is not until a Ms. is completed—roughly—that one can actually tell where it is balanced, and where it is light-weight or top-heavy. Things expand in unexpected directions as we go along; developments suggest themselves temptingly when we are halfway through, and then throw the earlier chapters quite out of proportion to the story as a whole; matters that seemed of great moment when we were in Chapter 2 have toned down to the very ordinary by the time we have piled on ten more chapters of stress and thrills and emotion.

One cannot stop to adjust it as one goes along, because no one can say whether the re-adjustment itself may not be out of gear by the time the finale is reached.

Consequently, the best way is to go right on, letting everything fall as it happens (but keeping as near as you can to your original plan, unless there is just cause for a departure therefrom). When you have written "Finis," overhaul the Ms. from beginning to end, sparing neither your blue pencil nor your feelings, if common sense, and knowledge of your craft, tell you that certain portions or sentences would be better omitted.

It is neither an easy nor a pleasing task—especially to the novice. The early children of our brain seem of such priceless worth, that we regard them with a certain sense of awe. "Did *I* write that beautiful passage about the moon silvering the tree-tops? Then it *must* belong just where I put it. Cut it out? Certainly not! I consider it the most exquisite paragraph in the whole story."

This is the way we look at our work when we have not many published items to our name. Later, experience and the training that comes from practice, teach us to arm ourselves as a matter of course with a blue pencil, ignore personal sentiment, and look at our Mss. with a coldly critical eye. Then we may discover that a sentence or paragraph, though of undoubted merit and beauty—(we need not deny it that much!)—does not quite fit in where we originally placed it. Possibly it is superfluous, in view of what follows later; or redundant, in view of what went before; or it may have lost life and colour with the passage of time; or it may seem hackneyed, or weak, (though we do not use such insulting words to our own writings till we are fairly advanced). But whatever the reason, if on examining a sentence, it does not appear to serve any vital purpose, take it out. If you think there is worth in it, save it for a possible use at a later date in some other Ms., though, personally, I do not believe in any sort of *réchauffé* of old matter, simply because as time goes on we change in our style of writing as we do in our tastes and preferences in neckties. And what you write this year, will not necessarily dovetail in with what you write in a few years' time. Still, if you feel it would be wasting flashes of genius to destroy it, and it would be any comfort to you to hoard it—do so; the main thing is to delete it from the Ms. you are revising, if there be any doubt about its value.

A beginner's Ms. usually needs to be cut down to about half its original length. Hard luck, for the beginner, I know, considering the way he will have laboured lovingly over every sentence.

MSS. NEED TO BE "PULLED TOGETHER"

Nevertheless, it pulls the work together if the blue pencil be applied generously. Some articles and stories appear to sprawl all over the place (sprawl is not a pretty word, but it is expressive). The writer does not seem able to follow up any idea to a logical conclusion, without interpolating so much irrelevant matter that the main theme is nearly smothered by the extraneous items, and the reader gets only a confused impression of what it is all about.

Such work needs "pulling together," *i.e.* the essential portions that should follow each other in natural sequence need to be brought closer together; and this can only be done by clearing away the non-essentials that separate them.

THE WAY PHIL MAY MADE HIS SKETCHES

The late Phil May once showed me how he drew his inimitable sketches, that always looked so simple, oh *so* simple! to the uninitiated. First he made a sketch full of detail, with everything included, much as other people make sketches. When this was finished to his satisfaction, he started to take out every line that was not actually necessary to the understanding of the picture. Finally he had left nothing but a few strokes—yet, such was his genius for seeing what to delete and what to leave, the picture had gained rather than lost in character, force, and comprehensiveness.

The secret of the matter is this. By removing everything that is not of vital importance to the whole, (whether in painting or in writing), there is less confusion of vision, less to distract the mind, or switch it off to side issues.

This does not mean that everything is better for being given in bare outline. Undoubtedly certain additions and decorations and descriptions can be made to emphasise the author's meaning, to impress a scene more vividly on the mind. We do not want all our pictures to be modelled on the lines of Phil May, clever as his work was. There is room for endless variety. The author should remember, however, that it is better to err on the side of drastic deletion, rather than leave in matter that is no actual gain to the picture, and only serves to distract and confuse and overload the reader's mind.

BEWARE THE PLAUSIBLE IMP

There is a Plausible Imp who perches on the top of every beginner's inkstand, and passes his wicked little time assuring them all that they are too clever to need hedging about by rules, that their work cannot be improved upon, and would only be spoilt if it were altered in any way.

Don't heed him! The beginner's work is never spoilt by condensation; rather it is invariably improved by cutting down. In the main, every writer's work needs pruning, until he has had sufficient practice to know what is not worth while to put down in the first place—and one needs to be exceptionally gifted to know this.

If, on reading your Ms. after its completion, you feel your work is so good that it needs no blue pencil—beware! You have not got there yet!

PART FIVE

Author, Publisher, and Public

Everything resolves itself down, in the publisher's mind,
to the one simple question:
"Is this Ms. what the public wants?"

When Offering Goods for Sale

Supposing—that when you go into the fishmonger's, he offers you a cod that is slightly "off"; and, while apologising for its feebleness, begs you to take it, as he has an invalid daughter suffering from spinal complaint, who needs a change at the seaside.

Or—that the assistant in the men's hosiery shop begs you to take half a dozen extra neckties, as he is anxious to buy the baby a much-needed pram, and his salary depends primarily on his commissions.

Or—that the sewing-machine agent, when sending around circulars, adds a devout hope, as a P.S., that you will purchase a machine, since he is anxious to increase his subscription to foreign missions.

Or—that the incompetent dressmaker beseeches you to take a garment that would fit nobody and suit nobody, because she has a widowed mother to support.

"Preposterous!" you say. "Such things would never occur."

And yet this is precisely what is happening every day of the year in the literary business!

Here are some sentences from letters accompanying Mss. sent to my office the week I am writing this.

"I should esteem it a great kindness if you could stretch a point in favour of my story, even though it may not be quite up to your standard (and I can see, on re-reading, that it has defects); but I am anxious to make some money in order to take a friend in whom I am deeply interested to the seaside for a much-needed change. She is an invalid, and—" here follow copious details about the friend.

Another writes: "I must ask you to give this every consideration, as I devote all the money I make by my writings to charity."

A third says frankly, "you really *must* accept this story, as I need money badly."

And for a truly nauseating letter, I think the following is as objectionable as any I have received in this connection:

"My dear wife has recently passed away, after years of acute and protracted suffering. My heart was rent with sympathy for her while she lived, and now the blank caused by her death is almost intolerable. How I shall face life without her I do not know; for she was indeed a help-meet in every sense of the word, In order to divert my mind from this well-nigh insurmountable sorrow, I have written a story 'The Forged Cheque,' which I feel is just the thing for your magazine. I ask you to regard it leniently, remembering that it is written with a breaking heart," etc.

The Problem of Youth

Then there are other reasons advanced why the editor should accept a Ms., the youthfulness or the inexperience of the author being frequently mentioned.

While it is no crime to be young, it is no particular advantage when one is seeking to place a story. Inexperience, on the other hand, might be regarded as a distinct drawback.

But in any case, the editor does not purchase Mss. merely because they are the writers' first attempts. However good they may be for first attempts, or however promising they may be considering the age of the writer, all that has practically nothing to do with the editor's decision, unless he is running any pages in his periodical for the exploitation of immature work or juvenile effort. And in these days of high-priced paper and expensive production, very few papers do this.

THE WAY PHIL MAY MADE HIS SKETCHES

It is hard to make the amateur understand that a magazine is first and foremost a business proposition, as much as a shop or a factory. The editor must make it pay; and in order to do this, he must publish the type of matter that his readers are willing to purchase. Each magazine appeals to a definite section of the public (or it should do so, if it is to be a success). No one magazine appeals to every human being. Some want sensation, some want art, some want fashions, and so on. And as it is impossible to include everything in any one publication, each editor aims to please a certain class of tastes—good, bad or indifferent, according to the policy of his paper. And he knows to a fraction almost, what will suit his public, and what they will not care about.

How does he know?

It is part of his mental and business equipment: the knowledge often costs him years of study and observation; and it is one of the qualifications for which he is paid his salary.

And because he knows what his public will buy, and what they do not want, he purchases Mss. accordingly. It is immaterial to him whether the writer needs money for charity, or to support an aged relative, or merely to soothe a bereaved soul: the only question he considers is whether the public will want a certain Ms. or not. He is not engaged by the proprietors to aid charity, or to minister to the necessitous; his work is to provide goods that the public will buy—just like any other business man. And he is unmoved, therefore, by irrelevant appeals.

Of course he has other matters to look to as well as the providing of goods the public will buy; he helps to shape public opinion, for instance, and raises, or lowers, the public taste. But so far as the amateur is concerned, the point to remember is the fact that an editor is in no way influenced by the writer's need for pecuniary assistance. If he were, his post-bag would be a hundred times heavier than it is already, and it is quite heavy enough as it is!

A PUBLISHER IS NOT AN AGENT FOR PHILANTHROPY

In the same way, only more so, a publisher is concerned with the selling qualities of a Ms. rather than with the writer's private affairs. He is running a business concern with a view to some margin of profit. Presumably he has a wife and family to support, rent, rates and taxes to meet (in addition to helping to pay for the war)—like any other man. And he spends his days in the dim, fusty airlessness of a publisher's office for the purpose of making a living out of the books he publishes. Therefore, he is not likely to be inclined to bring out a book, which his business experience tells him the public will never buy, merely because (as one sender of a Ms. recently put it) "the moral of my essays is really beautiful, and it will do people good to read them, if even they do not bring in profit. Read them yourself and you will see that I am not exaggerating."

Possibly the moral of a Ms. is quite good: but it may not be the particular brand of goodness that the public is willing to purchase at the moment; and the publisher knows it is hopeless to put it on the market in that case.

Equally it is useless to expect him to be influenced favourably simply because your earnings are ear-marked for charity. At the end of the year, should he see that the money he paid for a certain item was a dead loss, it would be no consolation to him to remember that the author had devoted the cash to a "Seaside Holiday Home for Men on Strike" in which she was interested.

Therefore spare him all such data. The less you add to what he has to read daily, the better. An accompanying letter is really unnecessary—only it is useful to affix the stamps to, for the return of the Ms. if rejected.

Profuse explanations are all beside the mark, and give an amateurish, unbusiness-like look to a communication. Whatever you may write about yourself on your Ms., in praise thereof, or in extenuation, everything resolves itself down—in the publisher's mind—to the one simple question: Is this what the public wants?

WE THINK WE CAN JUDGE THE VALUE OF OUR WORK BETTER THAN A PUBLISHER CAN

Many a beginner is convinced his Ms. would sell, if only it were printed. It is natural that we have a certain amount of belief in our own work, more especially if we have given much time and thought to it. Moreover, we possibly see points in it that no one else can; we see what a we meant to put down, without in any way realising how far our actual writing falls short of the ideas that were in our brain. The outcome of this partiality for our own writing, is a certainty that people are not able to do us justice if they do not think as highly of it as we do.

But the publisher is better able to judge of the selling possibilities of a work than the author; it is his business; he is at it all day long. He has no personal feelings involved, his main concern being to make a book a profitable concern; and his experience teaches him pretty accurately what the public will buy and what it will leave on his hands. He may occasionally make a mistake (though it is surprising how seldom an expert publisher does make a wrong estimate, considering how various are the Mss. that pass through his office); but when he does, he more often errs on the side of being over-sanguine, and giving the author the benefit of the doubt, than in the direction of turning down anything that might have made his, and the author's, fortune.

A CONSOLING THOUGHT—NO DOUBT

Some writers are convinced that the style of their Ms. was too good for the editor who rejected it, and altogether above his intelligence. This is a consoling thought, no doubt; but unfortunately it does not take one any further.

I know that instances are occasionally quoted (always the same instances, by the way), where books that ultimately achieved some success were declined by several publishers before they were finally landed. But in some of these cases the books in question were so very much off the beaten track as to be verging on freakishness—and no one living can guarantee a forecast of how the public will receive a freak! Here and there one finds a publisher who enjoys a gamble, and will risk a little on such uncertainties; (sometimes he gets his reward, more often he doesn't); but the majority prefer a safer, even though less exciting, course!

One other matter may have contributed to the refusals these Mss. met with— possibly they were offered to publishers who did not handle that particular type of work. Publishers usually specialise in fixed directions, just as magazine editors do. No one attempts to cover the whole range of reading; a glance at any publisher's catalogue will show this. A Ms. turned down by one, as being useless to the section of the public in which he is interested, may be taken by another, who reaches a totally different class of reader.

Therefore do not despair, if your story does not get accepted the first time of asking. There may be a variety of reasons why that particular publisher or editor did not want that particular Ms.

But in any case, don't sit down at the first rebuff and say, "What's the good of anything? A genius has no chance nowadays any more than poor Chatterton had!" (By the way, I have heard several desperate, would-be authors mention Chatterton and liken their own predicament to his, but not one has ever chanced to be able to quote me a line of his work!) There is no need to feel that the bottom has dropped out of the universe, because your Ms. has been returned. Try elsewhere.

If it is declined by five or six different publishers, then you may safely conclude that it is not the kind of work the public will buy at the moment; or it may be that your writing is not sufficiently mature. In that case, put that Ms. aside, and tackle another, something quite fresh. I never think it is worth while to try and re-write or re-construct the rejected Ms.—at any rate, not till you are tolerably advanced. It really takes no more time to write something entirely new.

"If only I could get an introduction to an editor, I am sure I could get my work taken." One often hears this said. Yet there never was a greater delusion than this idea that introductions work the oracle. It would be a different matter if an editor, or publisher, had a surfeit of good work, and really did not know what to discard: in such circumstances (which won't occur this side of the millennium!) an introduction might help to secure attention for an individual writer.

But as it is, the editor is only too anxious to purchase good work when it comes his way; he does not wait for any introduction. If a Ms. strays into his office that possesses the qualities he is looking for, he writes the author forthwith, his one desire being to purchase the Ms.

Still, if you really feel you must be armed with some such document, it is as well to be quite sure that the introduction is a desirable one. Here are two letters that reached me by the same post.

The first was from Miss Blank, a stranger, who said—

"My friend Mr. Dash, who thinks *very* highly of my work, has *urged* me to let you see some of it, as he thinks it is just the sort of thing you will be glad to have for your magazine. He is writing a letter of introduction. I shall be glad if you will name a time for a personal interview, as I can better explain"—etc.

The second was from Mr. Dash, an acquaintance of long standing, who said—

"There is a certain Miss Blank who is anxious I should write her a letter of introduction to yourself—which I do herewith. I know nothing whatever about her, save that she seems to be a first-class nuisance. I have never seen her, haven't a ghost of a notion if she can write: probably she can't. But she happens to be the sister of the fiancé of the daughter of my mother-in-law's dearest and oldest friend; and any man who values the peace and happiness of his home endeavours to propitiate his mother-in-law, especially when she has mentioned the matter six times already. Therefore I trust this introduction is in order."

Personal Interviews are seldom desirable as a Preliminary

The desirability of a personal interview with an editor is another delusion to which the amateur clings. As a rule nothing is gained (but a good deal of time is lost) by talking a contribution over before the preliminary Ms. is read. After all, the Ms. is the item by which the author stands or falls. If it is good, and what the editor wants, he will take it—and take it only too gladly; if it is not good, or not what he wants, no amount of preliminary conversation will secure its acceptance; for no matter how delightful the conversation may have been, he does not print that; it is the Ms. itself that decides the crucial question of publication or no publication.

In some cases a preliminary letter is desirable: it may be advisable to ascertain beforehand whether an editor is open to consider an article on a doubtful subject. But if you wish to avoid inducing a sense of irritation in his soul, do not ask for a personal interview, since in all probability, if he is as rushed as most editors are nowadays, he will turn down the matter forthwith, rather than spend time on talk that may lead nowhere.

It must always be borne in mind that these are overworked, understaffed, hustling times in a very complex age; and the newspaper and magazine office feels this more keenly than any other branch of the business world, simply because periodicals must reflect the spirit of their day and generation, and keep the readers in touch with all that is going on,—and "all" is a large, and constantly changing, order at present. This means that the editorial offices are always more or less in a state of tension; there is no time to spare for interviews that may prove fruitless; the day is seldom long enough to get in all that is certain to be profitable to the paper.

Therefore, say what you have to say by letter—and say it clearly and briefly. The editor forms his judgment by what you say, and if he wants to talk the matter over with you, he will soon let you know.

"But I always feel I can explain myself so much better in a conversation—no matter how brief—than in a letter." This is a frequent plea.

The public, however, will judge you by what you write, not by what you say; if you cannot express yourself well in writing, you may speak with the tongues of men and of angels yet it will avail you nothing where the publication of your Ms. is concerned. If you cannot write about it so that the editor can understand, the public are not likely to be able to comprehend it any better.

Women are particularly prone to ask for an interview, and this because they instinctively rely to some extent on the appeal of their personality in most of their business transactions. By far the wiser course, however, is for a woman to express herself so well in her writing that the office simply tumbles over itself in its anxiety to make her personal acquaintance. And I have known this to happen on more than one occasion.

THE IRREPRESSIBLE CALLER

Nevertheless, men can also distinguish themselves when making calls. The card of a stranger, bearing a Nebraska address, was brought to me one afternoon. He urged that his business was of great importance. Finally I saw him. He was a most intelligent-looking American, and, like the majority of his countrymen, was not long in coming to the point. He said he had written some poems, and promptly placed before me a sheaf of Ms. I told him I would look at them if he would leave them.

"Just you run your eye down these," he said. I protested that I could not possibly do his work justice if I skimmed it in any such manner. Then he explained that these were not poems—the masterpieces would come later—these were press notices of some poems he had had printed in a Nebraska paper. I read a few; I had never even heard of the majority of the papers that reviewed his work; but he seemed to take himself very seriously, one had not the heart to shatter his illusions.

Then he produced the bales of poems. He watched me so eagerly I was obliged to read some. I besought him to leave the rest with me, as I could not decide so important a matter hurriedly.

"Oh, but just read this one," he persisted. "Mr. Blank of our city—never heard of him? You *do* surprise me!—he says he considers it as fine as anything your Percy B. Shelley ever wrote." In a moment of abject weakness I said the poem was fair. Then the heart of that man warmed towards me; he told me of his hopes, his plans and his aspirations, and I tried to sympathise with them. I could not do less, since I owe America much for kindness and hospitality it has shown me on many occasions.

When at last he rose, reluctantly (he had stayed an hour and a quarter), I offered him my hand. He took it with a hearty grip.

"Well, I'm real glad to have known you," he said. "It's been a genuine pleasure to have this talk with you, for you are, without exception, the most informed and intellectual person I've met since I've been in your country." I felt immediately remorseful that I had grudged him the little chat; he was evidently a discerning young man.

"The pleasure has been mine," I assured him, and inquired how long he had been in England? "I landed at Southampton at ten o'clock this morning," was the response. I smilingly tried to disguise the sudden lapse of my enthusiasm. I must have succeeded, for he next said:

"And now I guess I'll go down and fetch up my wife. She's been waiting in the street outside while I came up to see what you were like. I size it she'll just enjoy making a little visit with you."

Mss. cannot always be Read as Soon as they are Received

It is only natural that an author should be keen to know the verdict on his work, once he has sent it out to try its fortune. But it is useless to get impatient because no news of it is forthcoming next day. Sometimes weeks elapse, sometimes months, before a Ms. can be read. But since the publisher makes no charge for reading a Ms. (and the reading costs money: some one's time has to be paid for, and it is some one who draws a fair salary, too), he must be allowed to do it at his own convenience. If he has not asked you to send a Ms., you cannot exactly dictate how soon it should be read.

Naturally, it is read as quickly as possible; this is to every one's interest; but this does not mean that it can be read the next day, or even the next week. Other authors may have preceded you.

The amateur who sends letters of inquiry before one has scarcely had time to open the envelope, is doomed to have his work rejected. No office has time to write and explain that "the matter will be considered in due course," etc., so the Ms. is merely returned.

It seems impossible to make the average beginner understand that his is not the only story offered, and that things have to take their turn.

Moreover, it is as difficult to please everybody as it was for the old man with the donkey in the fable. If Mss. are not returned immediately, the editor is bombarded with complaints from one set of aggrieved authors; if he is able to read them at once, and he returns them quickly, he is the recipient of uncharitable letters accusing him of having discarded the Mss. unread.

There is an interesting story of a suspicious lady who prided herself on laying traps for the negligent editor—pages put in the wrong order, others upside down, and suchlike devices with which every magazine office is familiar. At last she succeeded in proving that the monster who sat at the receipt of Mss. in one particular publishing house was a consummate rascal.

"SIR," she wrote, "I have long suspected that you basely deceive the public into believing that you read their works, while in reality you return them unread. But at last I have caught you hot-handed in the very act. It will doubtless interest you to know that I purposely gummed together pages 96 and 97, very slightly, in the top right-hand corner. Had you fulfilled your duty and done the work for which your employer pays you a salary, you would have discovered this and detached the pages in question."

The editor replied:

"DEAR MADAM,—If you will take a sharp pen-knife, and remove the fragment of gum between pages 96 and 97, in the top right-hand corner, it may interest you to discover my initials underneath."

IF YOU WISH YOUR MS. TO BE READ: MAKE THE READING EASY

"Should all Mss. be typed?" is a question often asked.

It is advisable to have them typed if possible, as this enables them to be read more quickly than if sent untyped.* Remember that your object in sending a Ms. to a publisher, or editor, is to get it read: therefore it is policy to do all in your power to facilitate the reading.

Owing to the widespread interest in literature, and the universal desire to see oneself in print, the number of Mss. that reach the office of any general periodical of good standing, is immense; and the eye-strain entailed in reading is very great. It has therefore become necessary to ask for Mss. to be typed when possible; though anything that was clearly written, in a bold readable hand, would never be turned down because it was not typed. What is desired is that a Ms. shall be legible, so that it can be read with the least amount of detriment to the eyesight. Whereas some of the untyped work that is sent is a positive insult. I have seen tiny, niggling writing, crossed out and re-crossed out, till even the compositor (who is a perfect genius for reading the utterly illegible) could scarcely have made it out. And in all probability, such a Ms. would be not over-clean, and would be *rolled* to go through the post.

WHY EDITORS DO NOT CRITICISE

"If you are unable to make use of my Ms., I shall be glad if you will kindly criticise it, and tell me exactly what you think of it."

This request is frequently made by senders of Ms. And when they receive

---

* *Publisher's Note: Now days, any manuscript not typed is not read.*

back their work without any comment they will write and say, "At least you might have sent one word by way of criticism. If you had only written 'good' or 'bad,' I should have some idea why you declined it."

I sympathise heartily with those who want advice; I know how very difficult it is to get any guidance or criticism that can be relied upon to be disinterested. Nevertheless, I wish the student could see the number of queries, and the amount of work, and the heap of Mss. that arrive at the office of any prosperous periodical; he would then begin to realise how utterly impossible it would be for Mss. to be criticised in writing. It would entail an extra staff, and an expensive staff at that, since such criticism is not work, like card indexing, that can be relegated to a junior clerk. Indeed, the sender of the Ms. would probably be highly indignant if any one but the editor did this work!

When I explain to beginners that we have no time to write criticisms on rejected work they say, "But it wouldn't take a *minute* to write down a few words, seeing that the Ms. has already been read."

Unfortunately, it would take a great many minutes. In any case it takes some time (if only a little) to sum up concisely the merits and defects of anything. More than that, experience has proved again and again that one little word of criticism will lead to more letters from the writer. And one has not time to read them! The children of our brain are very dear to us; and so sure as any one passes an adverse criticism on them, our feathers stand on end, and we prepare to defend our one little chick like the most devoted hen that ever lived.

Neither is it wise, I have found, to suggest a little alteration with a promise of publication attached. Two years ago I wrote to some one who had only had one short story published, indicating a new ending that would have improved her Ms. immensely, and made it possible for me to take it.

"My temperament requires that it shall end as I have written it. Kindly return my Ms. if you cannot use it," replied the lady loftily.

I did so.

Last week the same Ms. came back to me—much aged and the worse for wear—with a note that the author did not mind if I altered the ending as I had suggested. But two years is two years. And in the interval, while the Ms. was travelling round to every other office, the subject-matter had got out of date.

It is never politic to be touchy if by chance some misguided editor does offer a word of criticism!

If you want your work published, and there is no loss of principle involved, conform to the publisher's requirements as gracefully as you can, even though, in your heart of hearts, you consider him woefully lacking in discernment.

And you can comfort yourself, meanwhile, with the thought that when you are safely ensconced upon Olympian heights, you will even things up a little, and get back all of your own. I know one proprietress of several rejected Mss. who vows that whenever she "gets there," she will sit on the topmost pinnacle, and make all publishers and editors (including myself) walk up to her on their knees, dropping curtsies all the way!

A POPULAR DELUSION

I was making for my office one day when a sportive-looking girl stopped me on the stairs. "Just give this story to the editor will you, please?" she began. "Give it right into her hands, won't you; don't let any underling get hold of it."

I agreed.

"And—I say—just tell her from me that she's to read it *herself*, every word of it; I won't be put off with some assistant tossing it aside half read. I know their tricks."

One very popular delusion is that there is a conspiracy among the assistants in an office to keep Mss., and especially good Mss., from the eye of the chief! People will resort to all sorts of devices with the idea of ensuring Mss. reaching the editor's own hands. They are marked "personal," and "strictly private," or "please forward, if away"; and I had one endorsed, "Not to be opened by any one but the Editor."

Yet what is gained by all this, save a definite amount of delay? In any well-organised office, work has to follow a certain routine; Mss. have to be entered up by clerks as received, the stamps sent for return postage have to be checked and duly noted by the proper department, etc. Why delay the handling of the Ms. for a few weeks by having it so addressed that it may follow the editor to the North Pole, and back, before it is opened, if the endorsements were obeyed?—which of course they are not.

Let a Ms. take its proper course. No one in the office desires to suppress genius; on the contrary, great indeed is the elation of any member of the staff who discovers something worth publishing. It is one great object of our business lives.

A LITTLE TACT AND HOW MUCH IT IS!

If you feel you must call at an office in person, remember that the display of a little tact is a desirable accomplishment. When seeking a post on his paper do not start by telling the editor that his magazine is poor stuff, and will soon be on the rocks,—as I once heard a lady tell the editor of one of the most famous monthlies in existence. When he inquired as to her experience, it transpired that she had had one story—and one only—printed, and it had appeared in a child's magazine.

And it was another tactful caller who said, on leaving, after having absorbed five and twenty minutes of a busy assistant's time: "Well, perhaps you'll explain these suggestions of mine to the editor; though it would have been so much more satisfactory if I could have talked to some properly qualified individual."

Occasionally, however, a caller contributes something to the gaiety of nations, as in the case of the lady who came to inquire after the welfare of a Ms. she had left with some one in our building only the day before. (And, incidentally, she wanted to alter a word in it, as she had thought of one she liked better).

I was passing through the Inquiry Office as she entered, and she straightway explained to me her mission.

"I will find out who took it," I said, "I do not think you left it with me."

"Oh no! it wasn't you," she replied emphatically. "I left it with quite a nice-looking person!"

The Responsibility

The responsibility attached to the business of writing is greater than in any other department of work. The influence of the printed page is so far reaching, that no writer can gauge to what extent he may be furthering good (or harm), when he puts pen to paper.

You can calculate exactly an author's cash value by his sales: but this does not give an equally accurate estimate of his moral value.

Who would dream of measuring the influence of *Punch*, for instance, by the figures of its circulation? No one can say how many people will handle one single copy, or how many people will find in that single copy bracing laughter and healthy humour. The numbers printed each week can only represent a fraction of its actual readers.

And the same applies to a good many books: they pass from one to another, are borrowed from libraries, borrowed from friends (often without being returned, alas!), and by varied routes they penetrate to out-of-the-way corners of the world where the authors would least expect to be able to reach the inhabitants.

The most famous preacher living has not the possibilities of power that lie in the hands of a popular writer; and the gravity of this responsibility cannot be over-estimated.

While this does not mean that we must take ourselves too seriously, it does mean that we must take our work seriously, and recognise that it stands for something more than money-making, even though money-making is not to be despised.

To the beginner this may seem a weighty subject and rather outside his orbit. But in reality this point needs to be taken into consideration from the very earliest of our literary experiments. We must induce a certain attitude of mind, and keep definite ideals before us, if our work is to shape in any particular direction.

And the probability is that you will have to choose between good and ill when selecting the theme for your first story. You will naturally look around and study the type of fiction that seems to be selling well, and perhaps you may light on something peculiarly noxious, since there is an assortment of such books being published nowadays. The book in question may have been designated "strong" (the word reviewers often fall back upon, when they cannot find any adjective sufficiently truthful without being libellous, to convey an idea of a book's malodorous qualities!); or you may have heard the book lauded by people who make a boast of being modern, up-to-date, or advanced. And as we none of us aim at being weak, or old-fashioned, or behind the times, it is not surprising if the beginner feels that he, too, had better try his hand at something "strong," if he is to get a reputation for ultra-modernity.

Quite a number of novices choose unpleasant topics because, and only because, they fancy such themes show advanced, untrammelled thought, and "a knowledge of the world." They forget that of far greater importance than the extent of the writer's ability to defy the conventions, is the moral effect of a book on those who read it.

WIDER VIEWS ARE NEEDED WHEN CHARACTERISING LITERATURE

I use the word "moral" in its widest sense. It is unfortunate that we have got into the habit of pigeon-holing literature—and especially fiction—in very narrow compartments. When we speak of a book as "good," or "helpful," or "uplifting," we usually mean that it contains specific religious teaching in one form or another. Yet a book may be very good and helpful and uplifting without a single sermonic sentence, or anything approaching thereunto.

In the same way, when we say that a novel is undesirable or immoral, we generally mean that it deals with one particular form of evil: yet there are books having little or nothing to do with promiscuous sex relationships that are pernicious and unhealthy in the extreme, and possibly all the more dangerous because their immorality is not of the kind that is definitely ticketed for all to see, and beware of, if need be.

Everything tending to lower the tone of the soul is immoral; everything that debases human taste is unhealthy; everything that gloats on unpleasantness, for the mere pleasure of gloating, is as devastating as poison gas; everything that preaches a doctrine of hopelessness, that spreads the black miasma of spiritual doubt over the mind is bad—fiendishly bad.

But do not misunderstand me: I would not seem to imply that only fair things should be chronicled. There are certain facts of life that must be faced: sin cannot be ignored—but it must be recognised as sin, not be touched up with tinsel, and placed in the limelight, to look as attractive as possible.

Poverty, grime, sickness, gloom cannot be banished from every horizon; but they need not be dwelt upon exclusively without any alleviation, to the shutting out of all else. The wave of so-called "realism" that has swept over fiction of recent years has been a very injurious element in modern literature. It is bad from an artistic point of view, since it is one-sided, unbalanced, and not true to life itself, which invariably provides that compensations go hand in hand with drawbacks.

Some people speak of "realism" as though the only realities were sordidness and crime; whereas the earth teems with lovely realities—beauty of spirit, beauty of character, beauty of thought, no less than beauty of form and colour.

The slum at first glance does not look a pre-possessing subject; yet read "Angel Court": the writer who is a real artist can find gold even here!

ANGEL-COURT

By Austin Dobson

> In Angel-Court the sunless air
>   Grows faint and sick; to left and right
>   The cowering houses shrink from sight
> Huddled and hopeless, eyeless, bare.

Misnamed, you say? for surely rare
Must be the angelshapes that light
In AngelCourt!

Nay! the Eternities are there.
Death at the doorway stands to smite;
Life in its garrets leaps to light;
And Love has climbed that crumbling stair
In AngelCourt.

From *"London Lyrics,"* by permission.

Those who acclaimed these recent books of socalled "realism" as works of exceptional genius, did not see that, far from being any such thing, they were, in most cases, preliminary manifestations of a hideous malady, which has since culminated in all we understand by the word Bolshevism.

To dilate on ugliness, coarseness, harshness, without showing the counteracting forces at work, and to dabble continuously in dirt without showing the way to cleanliness, is not art, no matter how accurately every detail may be portrayed: it is merely systematised brutishness.

Even themes with a rightful motive may be exceedingly harmful under some circumstances. Studies of dipsomaniacs, drugvictims, and the like, may be necessary as matters of psychological or medical research, just as studies of any other diseases are necessary; but they should be issued as such, and not put forward in the guise of fiction intended for all and sundry among the general public.

I have enlarged on this matter, because there has been a great tendency on the part of amateurs lately to revel in descriptions of crudity and repulsiveness, with never a thought as to the effect of such literature on the reader. At no time is it desirable to circulate indiscriminately, much less as fiction, reading matter that can only induce morbidity, neuroticism, depravity, doubt, or depression. But in an age like the present, when most of the civilised world is bowed beneath an overwhelming weight of sorrow, shattered nerves and physical weakness, it is positively criminal to manufacture pessimism, gloom and horrors, and scatter this type of literature broadcast without any sense of the appalling responsibility attaching thereunto.

Qualities which cannot be Dispensed With

There are three qualities which all authors should aim to incorporate in their writings if they are to be a blessing rather than a curse to humanity: these are cleanness, healthiness and righteousness. They may be introduced in many and various forms; and are often to be found in wholesome laughter, spontaneous gaiety, good cheer, breathless adventure, revelations of beauty, as well as in direct appeals to the higher nature. Anything that will arouse sane emotions, and divert the mind from self, is to be welcomed as a benefaction in this world of many sorrows.

The late Charles Heber Clarke—better known to the public as "Max Adeler"—enjoyed great popularity at one time as a humorist. He was a man of strong religious convictions; and there came a day when he ceased to write his humorous pleasantries, seeming inclined to regard them as so much wasted opportunity. On one occasion however, a clergyman whom he met while travelling, on discovering his identity, grasped his hand and said, "You have made me laugh when there seemed nothing left to laugh about; you have helped me to get over some of my darkest days. I owe you more than I owe any other man in the world."

"And when he had finished pouring out his gratitude," said "Max Adeler," (who told me this himself), "I began to wonder whether, after all, one might not be doing as much good in the world by making people smile and forget their troubles, as by preaching at them."

To help humanity God-ward is the greatest privilege we can aspire to; but this can be done by other means besides the writing of hymns and commentaries. Everything that tends to lift humanity from the low-lands of sorrow or sordidness or suffering, and to point them to the great Hope; everything that will aid them to live up to the best that is in them, and to strive to recapture some long-lost Vision of the Highest, will be helping in the great work of human regeneration that was set on foot by the One who came to give beauty for ashes.

While only a few are entrusted with the message of the prophet or the seer, we all can specialise on whatsoever things are lovely and pure and of good report; and we shall be of some use—if only in a quiet way—to our day and generation if we can help others also to think on these things.

GOODNESS DOES NOT EXCUSE DULLNESS

But one point must not be overlooked—and in saying this I am summing up most that has gone before: If a book is to succeed, it must be well written.

Because a certain number of highly unpleasant books have succeeded, and a certain number of highly moral books have failed, beginners sometimes consider this as an indication of public preference. What they forget, or do not know, is this: The nasty book succeeded, in spite of its nastiness, because it was well and brightly written; while the moral book failed, in spite of its goodness, because it was badly written and superlatively dull. If the moral book that failed had been as well written as the nasty book that succeeded, it would not only have done as well as the nasty book, *it would have done a great deal better.*

All but a small degenerate section of the public prefer wholesome to vicious literature—but nobody wants a dull book! And the amateur writer of good books often overlooks this latter fact.

Therefore, bear in mind that it is not sufficient that you make a book clean and healthy and good; you must endeavour to make cleanness as attractive as it really is, and healthiness as desirable as it really is, and God-ordained Righteousness the most satisfying of all the things worth seeking.

When you can do this, you will find a fair-sized public waiting, and anxious, to buy your books.

You will not know what good you may be doing—it is never desirable for any of us to hear much on this score, humanity is so sadly liable to swelled head! But occasionally some one in the big outside world may send you a sincere "Thank you." When this comes you will suddenly realise, though you cannot explain why, that there are some things even more worth while than the publisher's cheque.

INDEX

D

Dante, why we read, 53.
David and Jonathan, 70.
Defects overlooked by fame, 57.
Delay in editorial decision on MSS., 121.
Delete superfluities in your Ms., 110.
dénouement, 97.
Dénouement as a surprise, 92.
Detail
　knowledge of, imperative, 12.
　study of, 48.
　too much, 43, 48, 64.
Devices to reach editors, 124.
Dialect
　an extra mental strain on reader, 85.
　requires exceptional skill, 86.
Diary form of story, 84.
Dickens
　central ideas of, 38.
Dickens, Charles
　an adept at "curtains", 100.
Diffusiveness, 50.
Divine discontent, 86.
Dobson, Austin, Angel Court, 126–127.
Does the public want it? The publisher's
　question, 117.
Dog, the real, 12.
Doll heroines, 14.
Dombey and Son in U. S. A., 100.
Dream Days, Kenneth Graham, 97.
Dreams of youth valuable,, 101.
Dressmaking and authorship, 3, 4.
Dull book not wanted by anyone, 128.
Dullness not necessary to goodness, 128.

E

Earle, Mabel, *Valley Song*, 107–108.
Eccentricity will not secure permanent
　interest, 57.
Editorial routine, 124.
Editors
　do not purchase Ms. because first at-
　　tempt, 116.
　have no time to criticise and advise,
　　123.

only buy what pays to publish, 116.
take time to read MSS., 121.
unmoved by irrelevant appeals, 115.
Eliot, Dr. Charles W., 32.
Emotionalism, 81.
Emotions of author not always interest-
　ing, 95.
Ending, a happy one best, 98.
Entertaining, every book should be, 59.
Environment and circumstances to be
　studied, 11.
Environment, your own, as your subject,
　87.
Every generation allows special character-
　istics of speech, 26.
Exclusive information necessary, 24.
Expressions, antiquated, 27–28.
Extracts, lavish use undesirable, 72.

F

Facts, ancient, to be omitted, 67.
Facts needed, 12.
Fame overlooking defects, 57.
Farnol, Jeffrey, and old-world "atmo-
　sphere", 81.
Feeding the brain with snippets, 21.
Fiction, monotonous character of Mss., 38.
Fiction, "strong", 125.
Field, Eugene, *Limitations of Youth*, 106.
"Fiona Macleod", 76.
First attempts in literature compared with
　art and music, 3.
First attempts rarely acceptable, 49.
First-hand knowledge, need of, 86.
First-person limitations, 83.
"Flower in a Crannied Wall,", 76.
Forest of Wild Thyme, Alfred Noyes, 108.
Form as applied to articles, 62.
Formless fragments, 74.
Fragments, 74.
Framework of story, 38, 39.
Freak writings cannot be forecasted, 118.

End

"The Lure Of The Pen"

Flying Chipmunk Publishing

FAIRY TALE COLLECTIONS
The Andrew Lang Fairy Book Series:

The Blue Fairy Book - 978-1-60459-547-5

The Green Fairy Book - 978-1-60459-549-9

The Crimson Fairy Book - 978-1-60459-759-2

The Violet Fairy Book - 978-1-60459-548-2

The Brown Fairy Book - 978-1-60459-758-5

The Orange Fairy Book - 978-1-60459-797-4

The Red Fairy Book - 978-1-60459-544-4

The Yellow Fairy Book - 978-1-60459-545-1

The Grey Fairy Book - 978-1-60459-756-1

The Pink Fairy Book - 978-1-60459-751-6

The Lilac Fairy Book - 978-1-60459-794-3

The OliveFairy Book - 978-1-60459-795-0

The Joseph Jacobs Folk and Fairy Tale Series:

English Folk & Fairy Tales - 978-1-60459-870-4

More English Folk & Fairy Tales - 978-1-60459-871-1

Celtic Folk & Fairy Tales - 978-1-60459-869-8

More Celtic Folk & Fairy Tales - 978-1-60459-876-6

Indian Folk & Fairy Tales - 978-1-60459-877-3

European Folk & Fairy Tales - 978-1-60459-878-0

Joseph Jacobs' English, More English & Indian Folk & Fairy Tales
978-1-60459-903-9 (Hardcover), 978-1-60459-895-7 (Paperback)

Joseph Jacobs' Celtic, More Celtic & European Folk & Fairy Tales
978-1-60459-904-6 (Hardcover), 978-1-60459-896-4 (Paperback)

Other Fairy Tale Collections

The Red Indian Fairy Book, by Frances Jenkins Olcott - 978-1-60459-753-0

The Japanese Fairy Book, by Yei Theodora Ozaki - 978-1-60459-754-7

Irish Fairy and Folk Tales, by William B. Yeats - 978-1-60459-796-7

COLLECTIONS FOR ADULTS AND CHILDREN

Halloween Games and Ghost Stories - 978-1-60459-483-6

Charles Dickens' Other Christmas Stories - 978-1-60459-488-1

Charles Dicken's Christmas Stories - 978-1-60459-490-4
  (*Collected from* Household Words *and* All the Year Round)

Thanksgiving, An American Holiday - 978-1-60459-750-9

Christmas, An AMerican Holiday - 978-1-61720-049-6

The One-Hoss-Shay, How the Old Hoss won the Bet, & The Broomstick
  Train, *by Oliver Wendell Holmes, Sr.* - 978-1-60459-872-8

Mr. Richard Hannay's War Adventures, *by John Buchan* - 978-1-60459-905-3
  (The 39 Steps, Greenmantle, & Mr. Standfast)

Ghost Masters, Volume 1 - Victorian ghost stories - 978-1-60459-486-7

Ghost Masters, Volume 2 - Victorian ghost stories - 978-1-60459-485-0

Flying Chipmunk Publishing

THE

Every Child Should Know

LIBRARY

FOLK & FAIRY TALES
EVERY CHILD SHOULD KNOW — 978-1-61720-115-8

"*Fairy Tales Every Child Should Know*" is a collection of twenty-four famous fairy tales from a wide array of classical works (Grimm's Fairy Tales, 1001 Arabian Nights, Hans Christian Andersen, and others). These tales are immortal and include: *The Enchanted Stag; Puss in Boots; Jack and the Beanstalk; The Princess on the Pea; The Ugly Duckling; Beauty and the Beast; Hansel and Gretel; Jack the Giant Killer; The Second Voyage of Sinbad the Sailor; The Story of Aladdin, or the Wonderful Lamp*, and many more. delightful tales. "*Folk Tales Every Child Should Know*" similarly pulls from the rich traditions of countries all over the world to deliver twenty classic stories such as: *Why the Sea is Salt; The Dragon and the Prince; The Story of Tom Tim Tot;* and *The Good Children.*

KIPLING STORIES & POEMS
EVERY CHILD SHOULD KNOW — 978-1-61720-116-5

Kipling is one of the most virile writers of our age. He lays India at our doors. He makes the jungle as attractive as a theatre. He is to India what Muir is to the great glaciers, what Lanier is to our southeast coast; what Burroughs is to our trees and forests and our serenity; what Cable is to the South; what Howells is to the psychology of The Boy; what Mrs. Custer is to army life and The Western Plains; what Markham is to Our Laboring Classes.

POEMS & FAMOUS STORIES
EVERY CHILD SHOULD KNOW — 978-1-61720-117-2

"*Poems Every Child Should Know*" is a collection of 187 famous poems from a wide array of classical and modern works, with such favorites as "*Twinkle, Twinkle, Little Star;*" "*The Owl and the Pussy-Cat;*" "*The Village Blacksmith;*" "*O Captain! My Captain!;*" "*How Sleep the Brave;*" "*Abide With Me;*" "*A Visit From St. Nicholas;*" and "*Ozymandias of Egypt.*" The authors include Clement Clarke Moore, Henry W. Longfellow, Robert Browning, Alfred Tennyson, Oliver Wendell Holmes, Sir Walter Scott, Rudyard Kipling, William Shakespeare, Walt Whitman and 94 others. "Famous Stories Every Child Should Know"is a collection of eleven stories by authors such as Charles Dickens and Nathaniel Hawthorne, including "*The Man Without a Country,*" "*The Great Stone Face,*" and "*The Story of Ruth.*"

MYTHS & LEGENDS
EVERY CHILD SHOULD KNOW — 978-1-61720-122-6

Flying Chipmunk Publishing

For Children 7 - 12
The Bobbsey Twins

by Laura Lee Hope

One of the longest running story series for children is *The Bobbsey Twins*. Follow the adventures of two sets of young twins at the turn of the Twentieth Century when there were no telephones, radios, and televisions, and horses and carriages were common. The twins enjoy wonderful days filled with sunshine and love with their playmates, Grace, Nellie, and Charlie, and get into and out of trouble as only little kids can manage. Their cat, Snoop, (and after book #4, "*The Bobbsey Twins at School*," their dog Snap, too) goes along on many of their adventures as they build snow houses, ice boats and kites, explore islands and boats, help their friends, and even save chickens from a flood! First published in 1904, each volume includes the original illustrations.

THE BOBBSEY TWINS, VOLUME 1 — 978-1-60459-980-0

The Bobbsey Twins, Merry Days Indoors and Out
The Bobbsey Twins in the Country
The Bobbsey Twins at the Seashore

THE BOBBSEY TWINS, VOLUME 2 — 978-1-60459-982-4

The Bobbsey Twins at School
The Bobbsey Twins at Snow Lodge
The Bobbsey Twins on a Houseboat

The Six Little Bunkers

by Laura Lee Hope

Another famous series is *The Six Little Bunkers*. Delightful stories for little boys and girls which sprang into immediate popularity when they first appeared in 1918. To know the six little Bunkers is to take them at once to your heart. Each story has a little plot of its own—one that can be easily followed—and all are written in a most entertaining manner. Join the fun, and mischief, as two parents try to keep track, and control, of six small children who are always exploring everything around them. Each volume includes the original illustrations.

THE SIX LITTLE BUNKERS, VOLUME 1 — 978-1-60459-983-1

The Six Little Bunkers at Grandma Bell's
The Six Little Bunkers at Aunt Jo's

THE SIX LITTLE BUNKERS VOLUME 2 — 978-1-60459-984-8

The Six Little Bunkers at Cousin Tom's
The Six Little Bunkers at Grandpa Ford's

Flying Chipmunk Publishing

Juvenile Stories for Teenagers!

The Moving Picture Girls

By Arthur M. Winfield

"*The Moving Picture Girls*" are the adventures of Ruth, age 17, and Alice age 15, DeVere, two young girls who live with their father, a widower and a theater actor, who is forced to leave his profession for the "Silent Movies." Both girls aid him in his work and visit the many localities these pictures are filmed at, as well as act in the movies themselves. This is what it was like when Hollywood was still a dream-in-the-making, and every stunt was performed live in front of a camera without computer-graphics. First published in 1914-15, each volume includes the original frontispiece illustrations.

The Moving Picture Girls, Volume 1 — 978-1-61720-028-1
...*First Appearances in Photo Dramas*
...*At Oak Farm–Queer Happenings While Taking Rural Plays*

The Moving Picture Girls, Volume 2 — 978-1-61720-029-8
...*Snowbound–The Proof on the Film*
...*Under the Palms–Lost in the Wilds of Florida*

The Moving Picture Girls, Volume 3 — 978-1-61720-030-4
...*At Rocky Ranch–Great Days Among the Cowboys*
...*At Sea–A Pictured Shipwreck that Became Real*

The Submarine Boys

by Victor G. Durham

A voyage in an undersea boat! What boy has not done so time and again in his youthful dreams? "*The Submarine Boys*" did it in reality, diving into the dark depths of the sea, then, like Father Neptune, rising dripping from the deep to sunlight and safety. Yet it was not all easy sailing for the Submarine Boys, for these hardy young "undersea sailors" experienced a full measure of excitement and had their share of thrills, as all who sail the seas are certain to do. The author knows undersea boats, and the reader who voyages with him may look forward to an instructive as well as lively cruise as The Submarine Boys fend off spies, saboteurs, and jealous rivals. First published in 1909, this volume includes the original eight illustrations.

The Submarine Boys, Volume 1 — 978-1-61720-031-1
...*On Duty–Life on a Diving Torpedo Boat*
...*Trial Trip–"Making Good" as Young Experts*

Flying Chipmunk Publishing

Juvenile Stories for Teenagers!

Uncle Sam's Boys

H. Irving Hancock

These stimulating stories are among the best of their class. They breathe the life and spirit of our army of today (or at least, as it was in 1910), and in which Uncle Sam's Boys fought with a courage and devotion excelled by none in the World War. This series tells the story of a soldier's life from the rookie stage until he has qualified for an officer's commission. First published in 1910-12, each volume includes the original illustrations.

Uncle Sam's Boys, Volume 1 — 978-1-61720-032-8
...In the Ranks–Two Recruits in the United States Army
...On Field Duty–Winning Corporal's Chevron

Uncle Sam's Boys, Volume 2 — 978-1-61720-033-5
...As Sergeants–Handling Their First Real Commands
...In the Phillippines–Following the Flag against the Moros

The Rover Boys

By Arthur M. Winfield

No stories for boys ever published have attained the tremendous popularity of this series. Since the publication of the first volume *"The Rover Boys At School"*, over three million copies of these books have been sold. They are well written stories dealing with the Rover boys in a great many different kinds of activities and adventures. Each volume holds something of interest to every adventure loving boy. This series, in fact, provided the template for other famous series such as the *Hardy Boys, Nancy Drew*, and *Tom Swift*, to name just a few. First published beginning in 1899, each volume includes the original illustrations.

The Rover Boys, Volume 1 — 978-1-61720-034-2
...At School–The Cadets Of Putnam Hall
...On The Ocean–A Chase For Fortune

The Rover Boys, Volume 2 — 978-1-61720-035-9
...In the Jungle–Stirring Adventures In Africa
...Out West–The Search For The Lost Mine

The Rover Boys, Volume 3 — 978-1-61720-036-6
...On the Great Lakes–The Secret Of The Island Cave
...In the Mountains–A Hunt For Fun And Fortune

Flying Chipmunk Publishing

Juvenile Stories for Girls!

Ruth Fielding

by Alice B Emerson

Ruth Fielding is an orphan who goes to live with her miserly uncle, Jabez Potter, and his housekeeper, Aunt Alvirah Boggs, who is "nobody's relative, but everybody's aunt." Uncle Jabez reluctantly provides for Ruth and never expresses any kind of love for her, while Aunt Alvirah loves her like a daughter. Determined to find her way in the world, this series chronicles Ruth's adventures and efforts to stand on her own and become independent of her uncle. First published in 1913-15, each volume includes the original illustrations.

Ruth Fielding, Volume 1 — 978-1-61720-037-3
...Of the Red Mill–Jasper Parloe's Secret
...Of Briarwood Hall–Solving the Campus Mystery

Ruth Fielding, Volume 2 — 978-1-61720-038-0
...At Snow Camp–Lost in the Backwoods
...At Lighthouse Point–Nita, the Girl Castaway

Ruth Fielding, Volume 3 — 978-1-61720-039-7
...At Silver Ranch–Schoolgirls among the Cowboys
...On Cliff Island–The Old Hunter's Treasure Box

The Meadow-Brook Girls

by Janet Aldridge

Follow the adventures of Grace, Harriet, Hazel and Margery, four young teenage friends from the New Hampshire town of Meadow-Brook, as they explore the outdoors and solve challenging mysteries. Starting with their first experiences at Camp Wau-Wau they find adventures and excitement. First published in 1913-4, each volume includes the original illustrations.

The Meadow-Brook Girls, Volume 1 — 978-1-61720-040-3
...Under Canvas–Fun and Frolic in the Summer Camp
...Across Country–The Young Pathfinders on a Summer Hik

The Meadow-Brook Girls, Volume 2 — 978-1-61720-041-0
...Afloat–The Stormy Cruise of the Red Rover
...In the Hills–The Missing Pilot of the White Mountains

Flying Chipmunk Publishing

Juvenile Stories for Teenagers!

The Radio Boys

by Allen Chapman

Written when radio was truly an unknown and exciting field of discovery, these stories follow the adventures of Bob, Joe, Herbert, and Jimmy as they build their own radio station, solve mysteries, and save ships at sea. First published in 1922, each volume includes the original illustrations.

The Radio Boys, Volume 1 — 978-1-61720-042-7
> ...First Wireless–Winning The Ferberton Prize
> ...At Ocean Point–The Message That Saved The Ship

The Radio Boys, Volume 2 — 978-1-61720-043-4
> ...At The Sending Station–Making Good In The Wireless Room
> ...At Mountain Pass–The Midnight Call For Assistance

The Radio Boys, Volume 3 — 978-1-61720-044-1
> ...Trailing A Voice–Solving A Wireless Mystery
> ...With The Forest Rangers–The Great Fire On Spruce Mountain

---

The Air Service Boys

by Charles Amory Beach

After learning to fly in America, Tom Raymond and Jack Parmly journey to France and tender their services to the Lafayette Escadrille, the French World War I air force. They go to the flying school of the French army and are taught the tricks of the famous French flyers. Then comes some thrilling services in the battle front. Written during World War I and first published in 1918, each volume includes the original illustrations.

The Air Service Boys, Volume 1 — 978-1-61720-045-8
> ...Flying for France–The Young Heroes of the Lafayette Escadrille
> ...Over the Enemy's Lines–The German Spy's Secret

The Air Service Boys, Volume 2 — 978-1-61720-046-5
> ...In the Big Battle–Silencing the Big Guns
> ...Over the Rhine–Fighting Above the Clouds

The Air Service Boys, Volume 3 — 978-1-61720-047-2
> ...Flying for Victory–Bombing the Last German Stronghold
> ...Over the Atlantic–The Longest Flight on Record

CLASSIC FICTION FROM CHARLES DICKENS

Oliver Twist, or, The Parish Boy's Progress—Oliver Twist, an orphan, escapes from a workhouse and joins a gang of pickpockets in London before being rescued. The novel is one of Dickens's best-known works. With the original George Cruikshank illustrations.   Softcover - 978-1-60459-484-3

A Tale of Two Cities—The story of two men, Charles Darnay and Sydney Carton, two cities, London and Paris, the French Revolution, and love. With the original illustrations of Hablot K. Browne (Phiz) and F.O.C. Darley. Charles Dickens' 17th novel.   Softcover - 978-1-60459-487-4

David Copperfield, or, The Personal History, Adventures, Experience, & Observation of David Copperfield the Younger, of Blunderstone Rookery—The most autobiographical of his novels "David Copperfield" follows the protagonist from childhood to maturity in the mid-1800's. Features the original 39 illustrations by Hablot Knight Browne (Phiz).   Softcover - 978-1-60459-489-8

OTHER FICTION

The Confidence Man, by Herman Melville—His last major novel and the first to portray that American icon - the con-man. More than just a thief, the con-man uses the victim's own greed (or desperation) to trick or trap the victim into giving the con-man what he wants.   Softcover - 978-1-60459-550-5

The One-Hoss-Shay, How the Old Hoss won the Bet, & The Broomstick Train, by Oliver Wendell Holmes, Sr.—One of the best regarded American poets of the 19th century. Here are three of his most famous poems. Features the original illustrations by Howard Pyle.   Softcover - 978-1-60459-872-8

Richard Hannay's War Adventures: The 39 Steps, Greenmantle, & Mr. Standfast, by John Buchan—One of the earliest examples of the "man-on-the-run" thriller, follows Richard Hannay, "an ordinary man" who puts his country's interests before his own safety during World War I.   Softcover - 978-1-60459-905-3

NON-FICTION WORKS OF INTEREST

Behind the Scenes – 30 Years a Slave, and 4 Years in the White House—The true story of the black slave Elizabeth Keckly, her meeting with the Lincolns, her experiences in the White House, and the sad end of her friendship with Mrs. Lincoln.   Softcover - 978-1-60459-808-7

Bundling & More About Bundling, by Henry Reed Stiles, M.D., and A. Monroe Aurand, Jr.—A curious custom, usually as a part of courting behavior—essentially, dating in bed. Originated either in the Netherlands or in the British Isles, and was common in Colonial America.   Softcover- 978-1-60459-543-7

Geronimo's Story of his Life, in his own words, by S.M. Barrett—One of the most feared Indians in the American Southwest, with 28 vintage photos.
                    Softcover - 978-1-60459-985-5

Look for the

FREE

Mother West Wind/
Peter Rabbit
Coloring Book

at

www.FlyingChipmunkPublishing.com
and Friend us on Facebook to see our latest releases!